IRON MAN ™

Believe

WRITER: KIERON GILLEN

PENCILER: GREG LAND

INKER: JAY LEISTEN

LETTERS: VIRTUAL CALLIGRAPHY'S JOE CARAMAGNA
COLOURIST: GURU EFX

ASSISTANT EDITOR: JON MOISAN
EDITOR: MARK PANICCIA
EDITOR IN CHIEF: AXEL ALONSO
CHIEF CREATIVE OFFICER: JOE QUESADA
PUBLISHER: ALAN FINE
EXECUTIVE PRODUCER: DAN BUCKLEY

COVER: GREG LAND

MARVEL
marvel.com
© MARVEL

TM & © 2013 Marvel & Subs. Licensed by Marvel Characters B.V. through Panini S.p.A. Italy. All ʀ██████ █████ █████hed by
Panini Publishing, a division of Panini UK Limited. Mike Riddell, Managing Direc██████████████████████ n Manager.
Marco M. Lupoi, Publishing Director Europe. Brady Webb, Reprint Editor. Ange███████████████████████
77 Mount Ephraim, Tunbridge Wells, Kent TN4 8BS. This publication may not b█████████████████████ the
condition that it shall not be sold or distributed with any part of its cover or ███████████████████taly.
ISBN: 978-1-84653-530-7 Do you have any comments or queries about this gra██████████████
Join our Facebook group at Panini/Marvel Grap█████

D0582551

MARVEL GRAPHIC NOVEL

IRON MAN #1

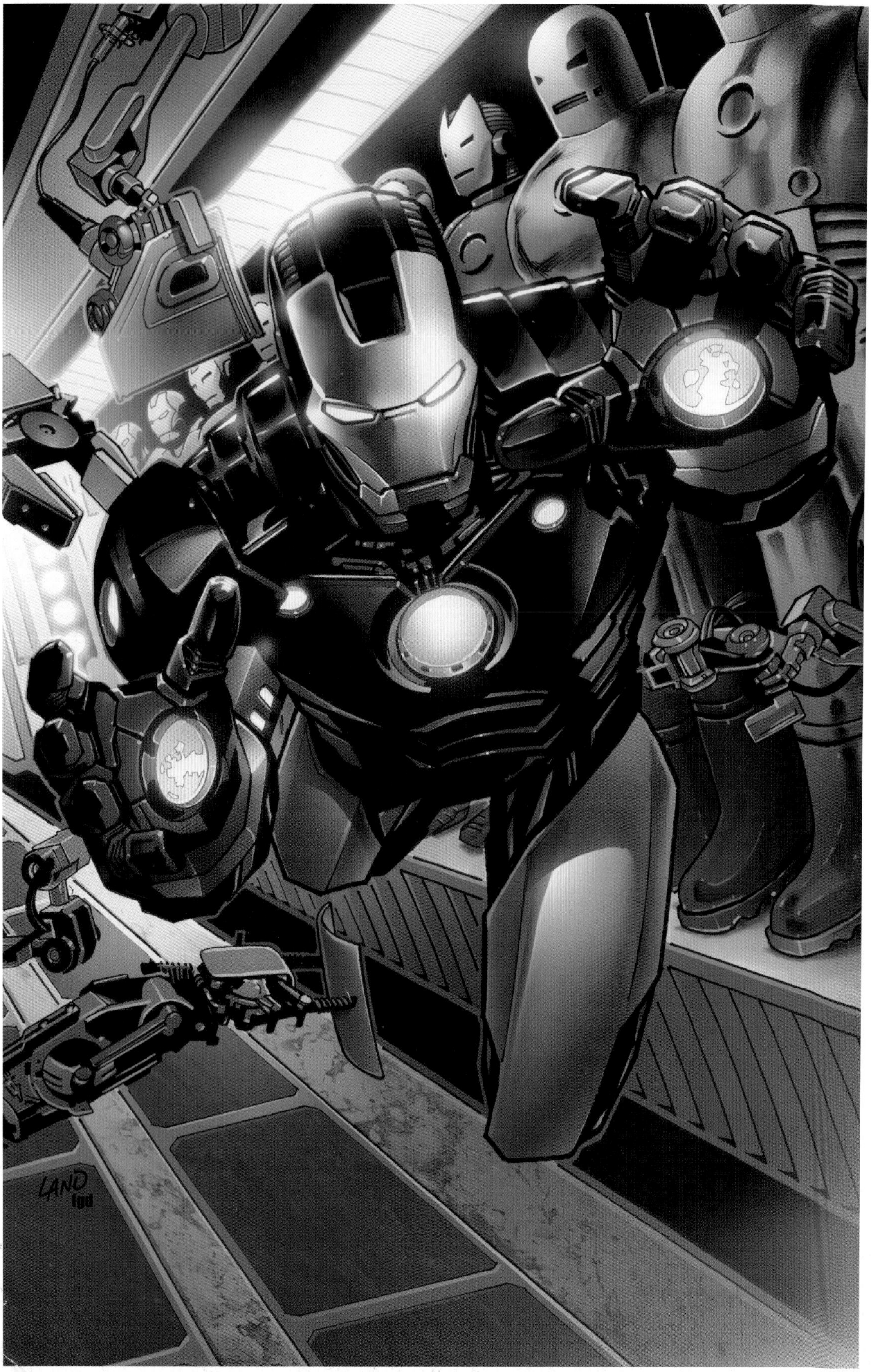
LAND
fgd

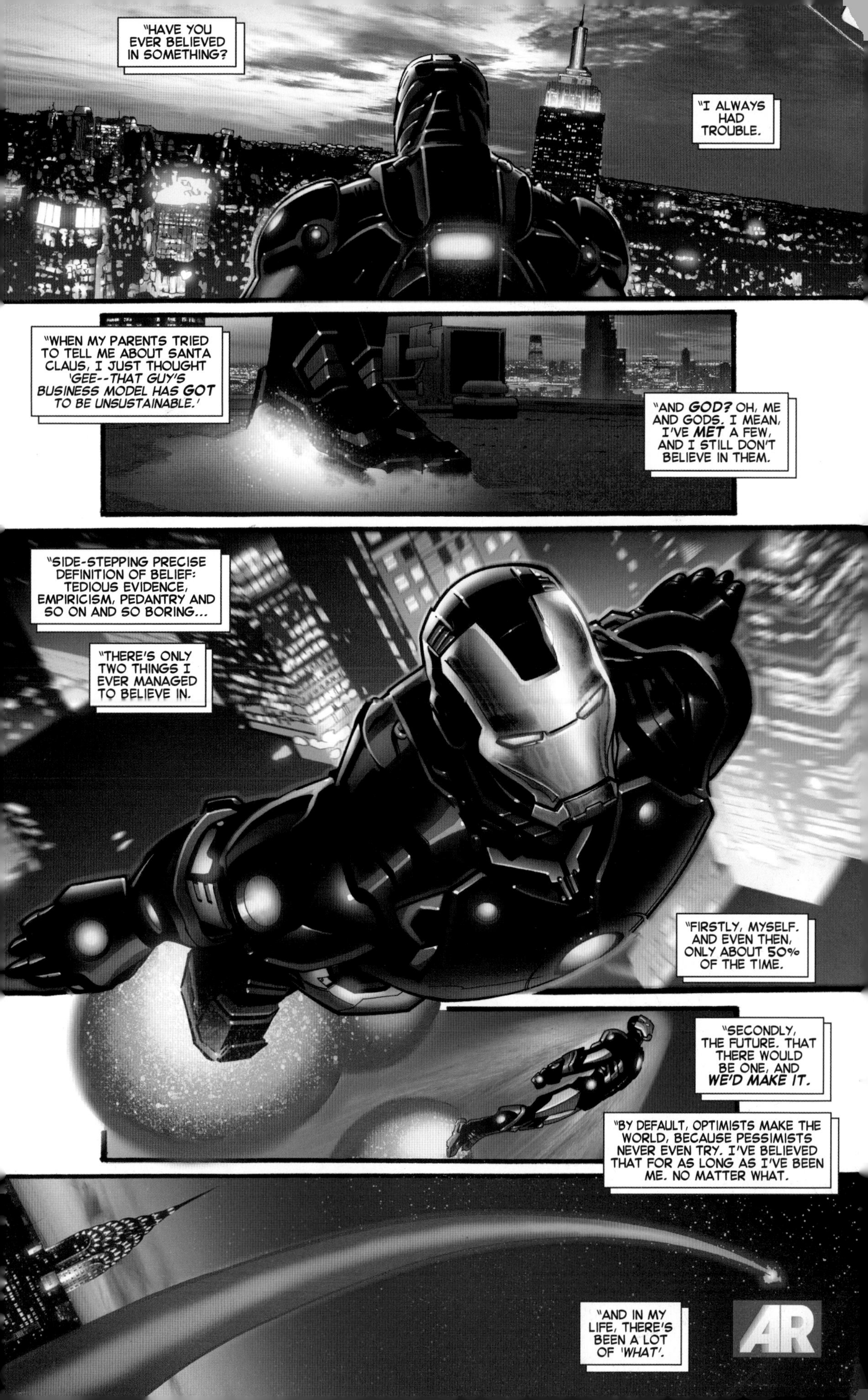
"HAVE YOU EVER BELIEVED IN SOMETHING?
"I ALWAYS HAD TROUBLE.
"WHEN MY PARENTS TRIED TO TELL ME ABOUT SANTA CLAUS, I JUST THOUGHT *'GEE--THAT GUY'S BUSINESS MODEL HAS **GOT** TO BE UNSUSTAINABLE.'*
"AND ***GOD?*** OH, ME AND GODS. I MEAN, I'VE ***MET*** A FEW, AND I STILL DON'T BELIEVE IN THEM.
"SIDE-STEPPING PRECISE DEFINITION OF BELIEF: TEDIOUS EVIDENCE, EMPIRICISM, PEDANTRY AND SO ON AND SO BORING...
"THERE'S ONLY TWO THINGS I EVER MANAGED TO BELIEVE IN.
"FIRSTLY, MYSELF. AND EVEN THEN, ONLY ABOUT **50%** OF THE TIME.
"SECONDLY, THE FUTURE. THAT THERE WOULD BE ONE, AND ***WE'D MAKE IT.***
"BY DEFAULT, OPTIMISTS MAKE THE WORLD, BECAUSE PESSIMISTS NEVER EVEN TRY. I'VE BELIEVED THAT FOR AS LONG AS I'VE BEEN ME. NO MATTER WHAT.
"AND IN MY LIFE, THERE'S BEEN A LOT OF *'WHAT'*.
AR

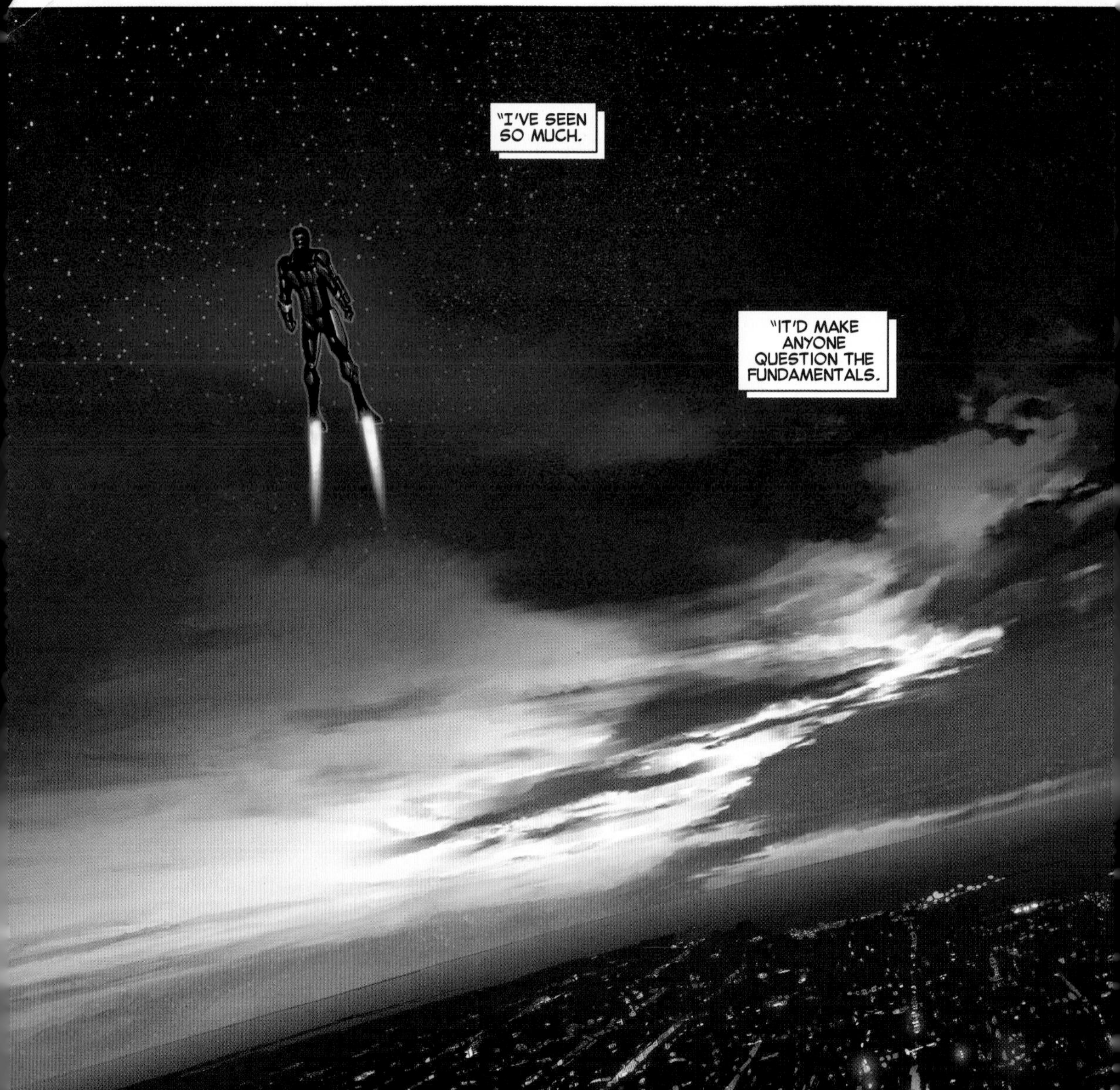
"I'VE SEEN SO MUCH.
"IT'D MAKE ANYONE QUESTION THE FUNDAMENTALS.

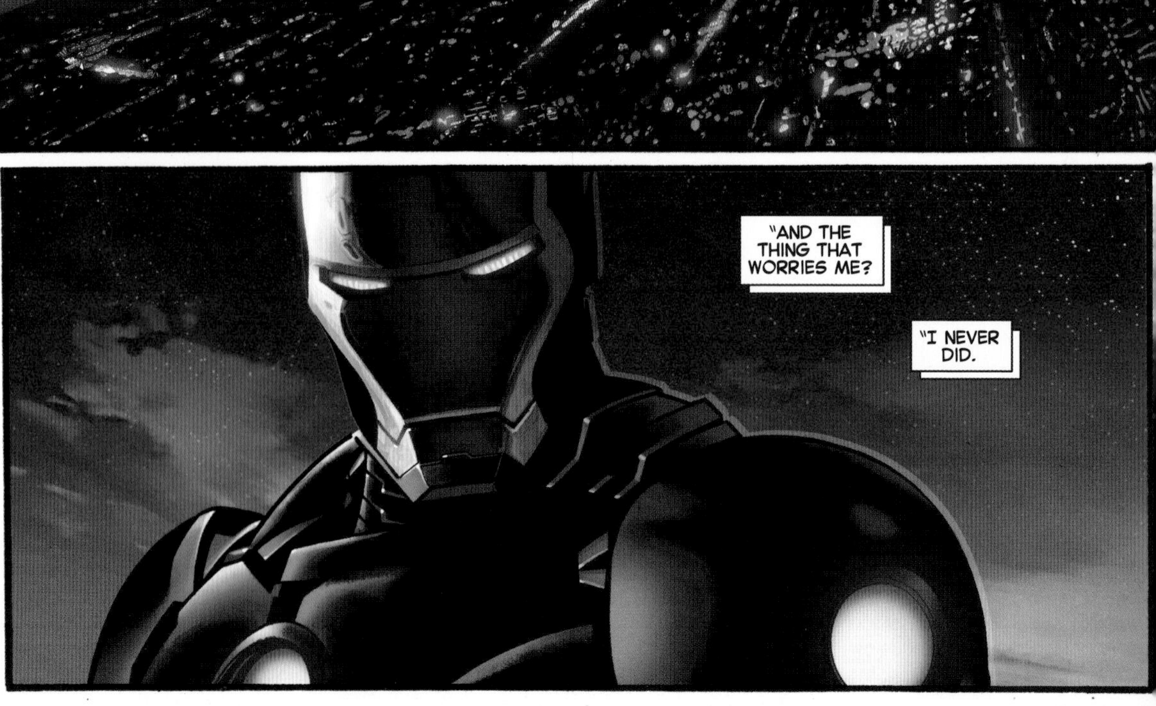
"AND THE THING THAT WORRIES ME?
"I NEVER DID.

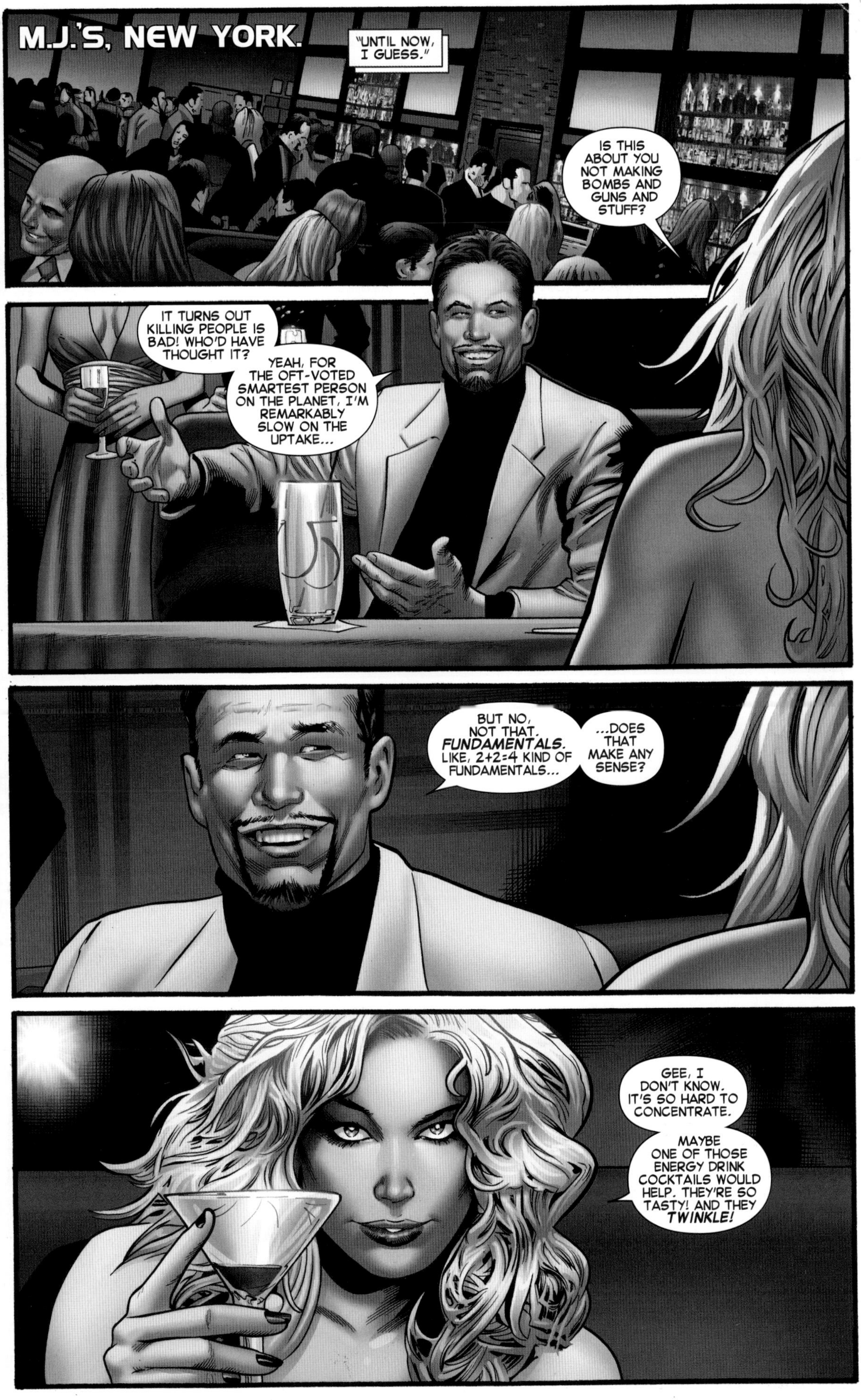
M.J.'S, NEW YORK.
"UNTIL NOW, I GUESS."
IS THIS ABOUT YOU NOT MAKING BOMBS AND GUNS AND STUFF?
IT TURNS OUT KILLING PEOPLE IS BAD! WHO'D HAVE THOUGHT IT?
YEAH, FOR THE OFT-VOTED SMARTEST PERSON ON THE PLANET, I'M REMARKABLY SLOW ON THE UPTAKE...
BUT NO, NOT THAT. FUNDAMENTALS. LIKE, 2+2=4 KIND OF FUNDAMENTALS...
...DOES THAT MAKE ANY SENSE?
GEE, I DON'T KNOW. IT'S SO HARD TO CONCENTRATE.
MAYBE ONE OF THOSE ENERGY DRINK COCKTAILS WOULD HELP. THEY'RE SO TASTY! AND THEY TWINKLE!

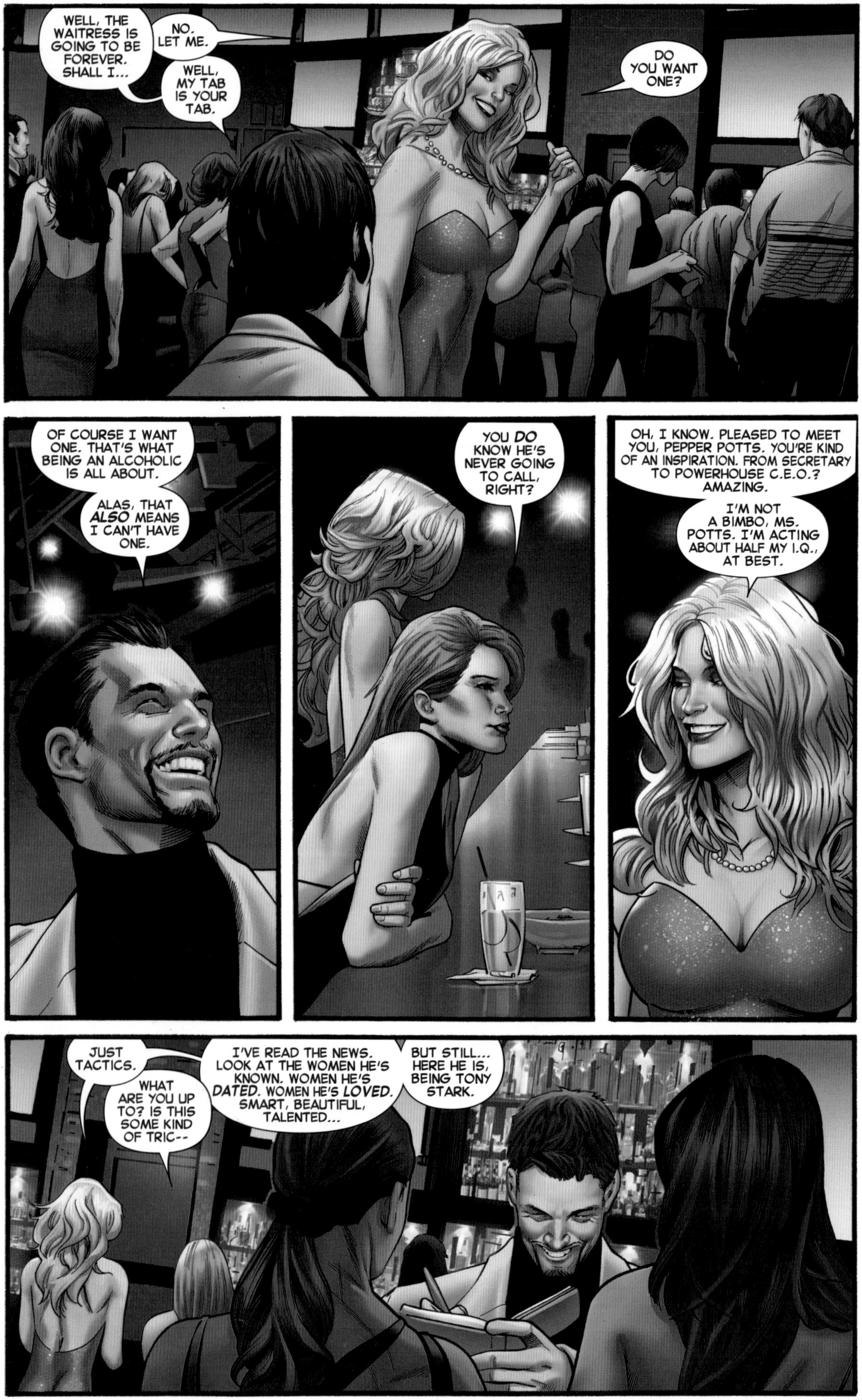
WELL, THE WAITRESS IS GOING TO BE FOREVER. SHALL I...
NO. LET ME.
WELL, MY TAB IS YOUR TAB.
DO YOU WANT ONE?
OF COURSE I WANT ONE. THAT'S WHAT BEING AN ALCOHOLIC IS ALL ABOUT.
ALAS, THAT ALSO MEANS I CAN'T HAVE ONE.
YOU DO KNOW HE'S NEVER GOING TO CALL, RIGHT?
OH, I KNOW. PLEASED TO MEET YOU, PEPPER POTTS. YOU'RE KIND OF AN INSPIRATION. FROM SECRETARY TO POWERHOUSE C.E.O.? AMAZING.
I'M NOT A BIMBO, MS. POTTS. I'M ACTING ABOUT HALF MY I.Q., AT BEST.
JUST TACTICS.
WHAT ARE YOU UP TO? IS THIS SOME KIND OF TRIC--
I'VE READ THE NEWS. LOOK AT THE WOMEN HE'S KNOWN. WOMEN HE'S DATED. WOMEN HE'S LOVED. SMART, BEAUTIFUL, TALENTED...
BUT STILL... HERE HE IS, BEING TONY STARK.

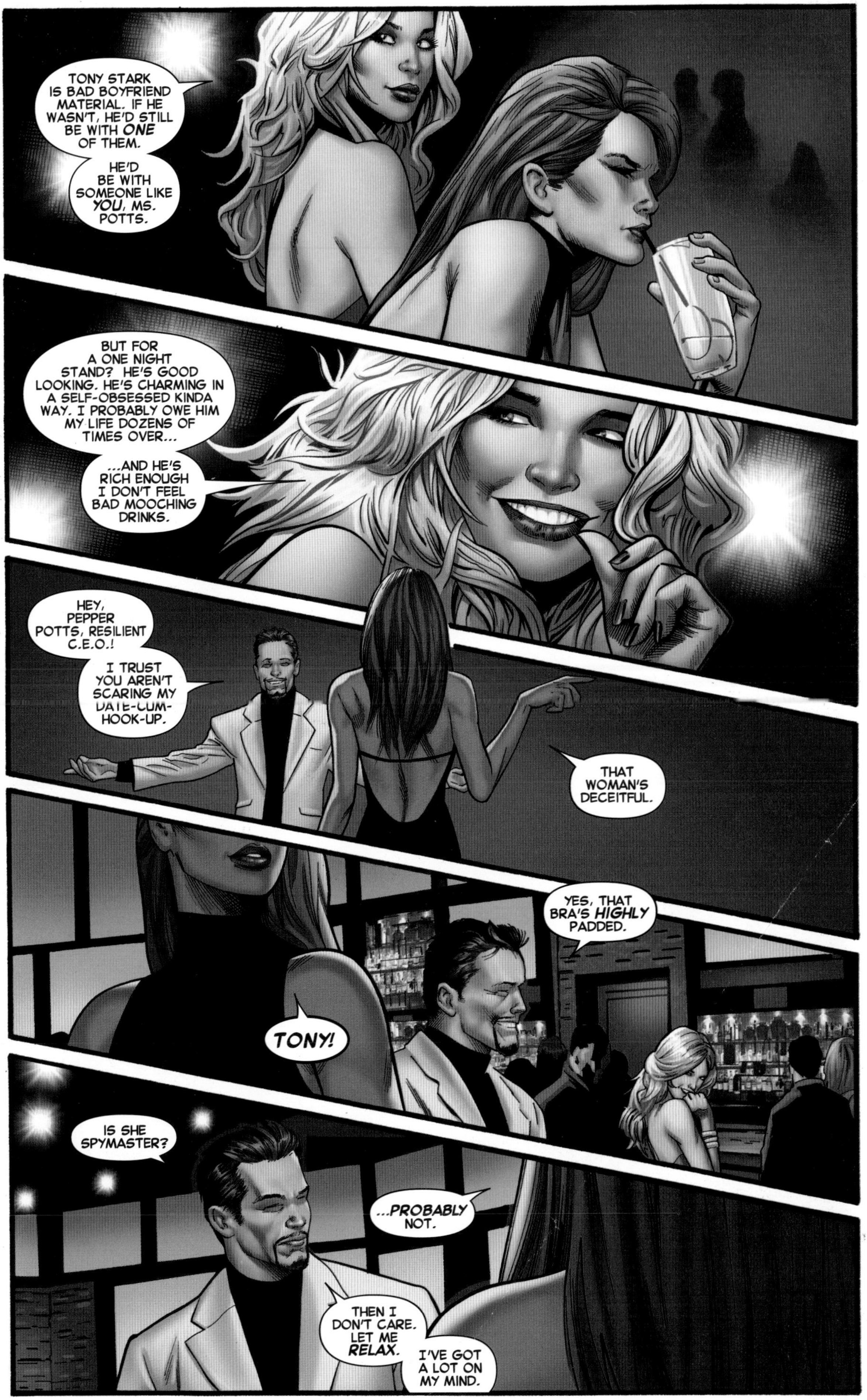

TONY STARK IS BAD BOYFRIEND MATERIAL. IF HE WASN'T, HE'D STILL BE WITH *ONE* OF THEM.
HE'D BE WITH SOMEONE LIKE *YOU*, MS. POTTS.
BUT FOR A ONE NIGHT STAND? HE'S GOOD LOOKING. HE'S CHARMING IN A SELF-OBSESSED KINDA WAY. I PROBABLY OWE HIM MY LIFE DOZENS OF TIMES OVER...
...AND HE'S RICH ENOUGH I DON'T FEEL BAD MOOCHING DRINKS.
HEY, PEPPER POTTS, RESILIENT C.E.O.!
I TRUST YOU AREN'T SCARING MY DATE-CUM-HOOK-UP.
THAT WOMAN'S DECEITFUL.
YES, THAT BRA'S *HIGHLY* PADDED.
TONY!
IS SHE SPYMASTER?
...*PROBABLY* NOT.
THEN I DON'T CARE. LET ME *RELAX*.
I'VE GOT A LOT ON MY MIND.

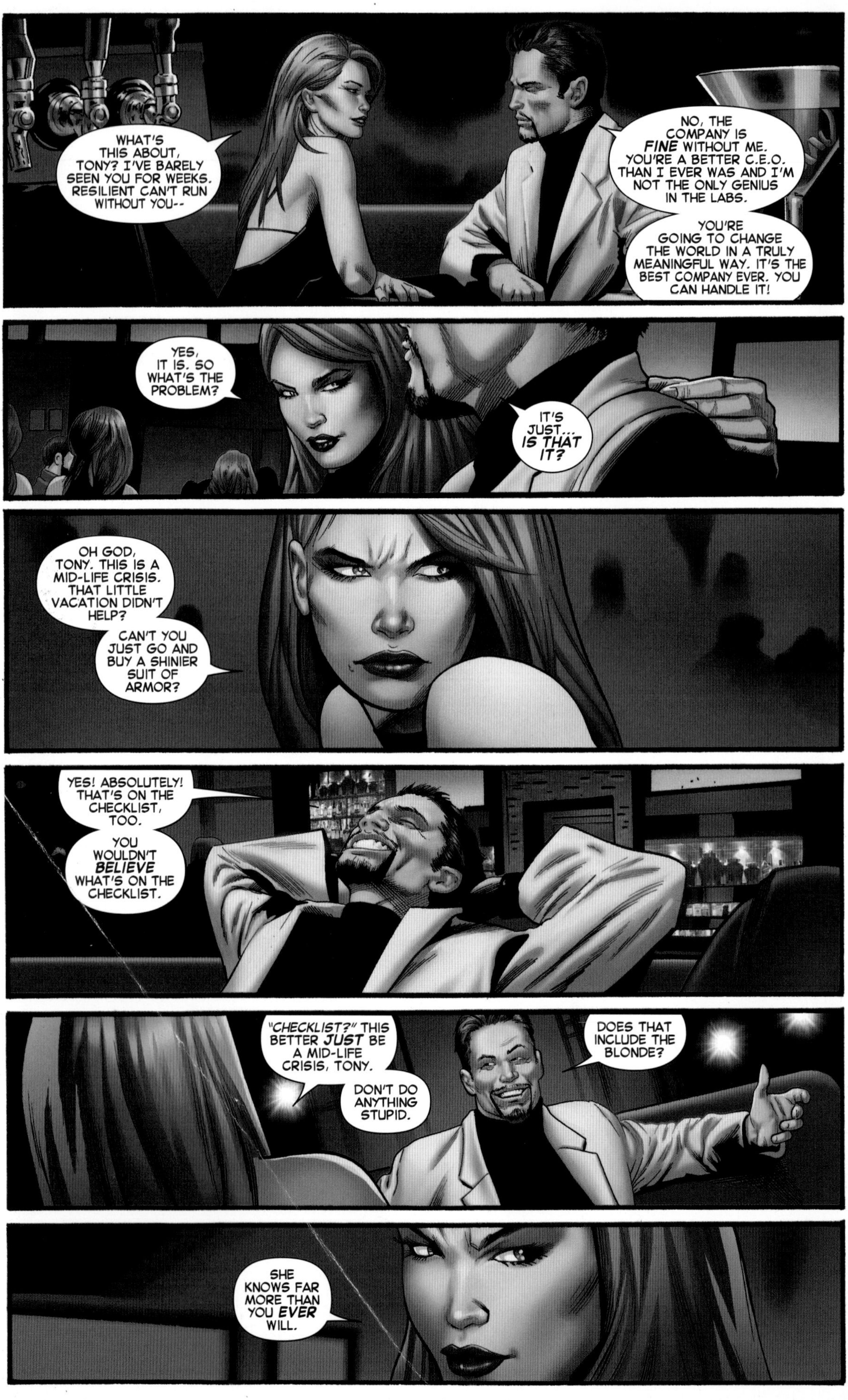
WHAT'S THIS ABOUT, TONY? I'VE BARELY SEEN YOU FOR WEEKS. RESILIENT CAN'T RUN WITHOUT YOU--
NO, THE COMPANY IS FINE WITHOUT ME. YOU'RE A BETTER C.E.O. THAN I EVER WAS AND I'M NOT THE ONLY GENIUS IN THE LABS.
YOU'RE GOING TO CHANGE THE WORLD IN A TRULY MEANINGFUL WAY. IT'S THE BEST COMPANY EVER. YOU CAN HANDLE IT!
YES, IT IS. SO WHAT'S THE PROBLEM?
IT'S JUST... IS THAT IT?
OH GOD, TONY. THIS IS A MID-LIFE CRISIS. THAT LITTLE VACATION DIDN'T HELP?
CAN'T YOU JUST GO AND BUY A SHINIER SUIT OF ARMOR?
YES! ABSOLUTELY! THAT'S ON THE CHECKLIST, TOO.
YOU WOULDN'T BELIEVE WHAT'S ON THE CHECKLIST.
"CHECKLIST?" THIS BETTER JUST BE A MID-LIFE CRISIS, TONY.
DON'T DO ANYTHING STUPID.
DOES THAT INCLUDE THE BLONDE?
SHE KNOWS FAR MORE THAN YOU EVER WILL.

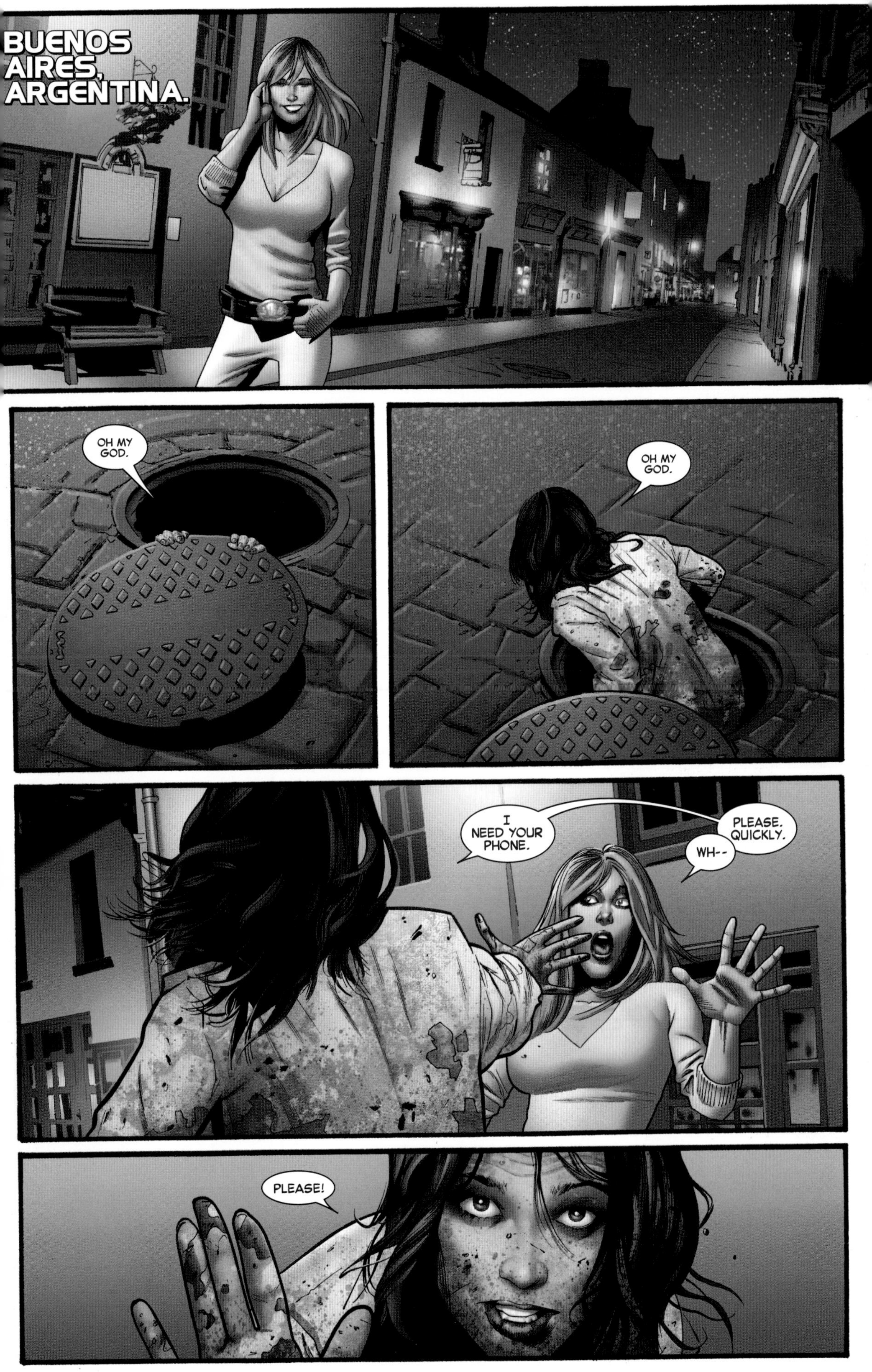
BUENOS AIRES, ARGENTINA.
OH MY GOD.
OH MY GOD.
I NEED YOUR PHONE.
WH--
PLEASE. QUICKLY.
PLEASE!

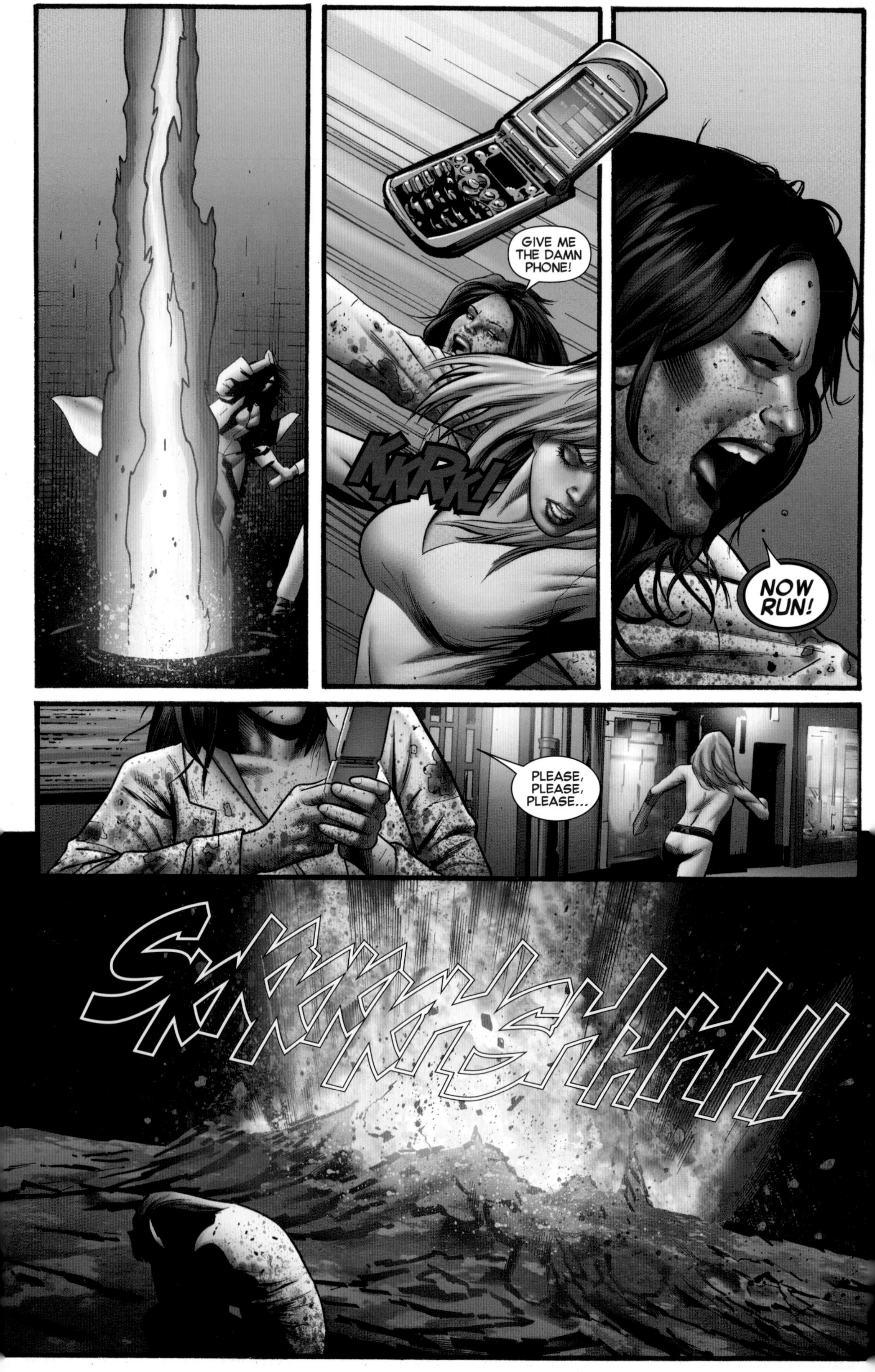
GIVE ME THE DAMN PHONE!
KKRK!
NOW RUN!
PLEASE, PLEASE, PLEASE...
SKRAAAKOOOOMMM!

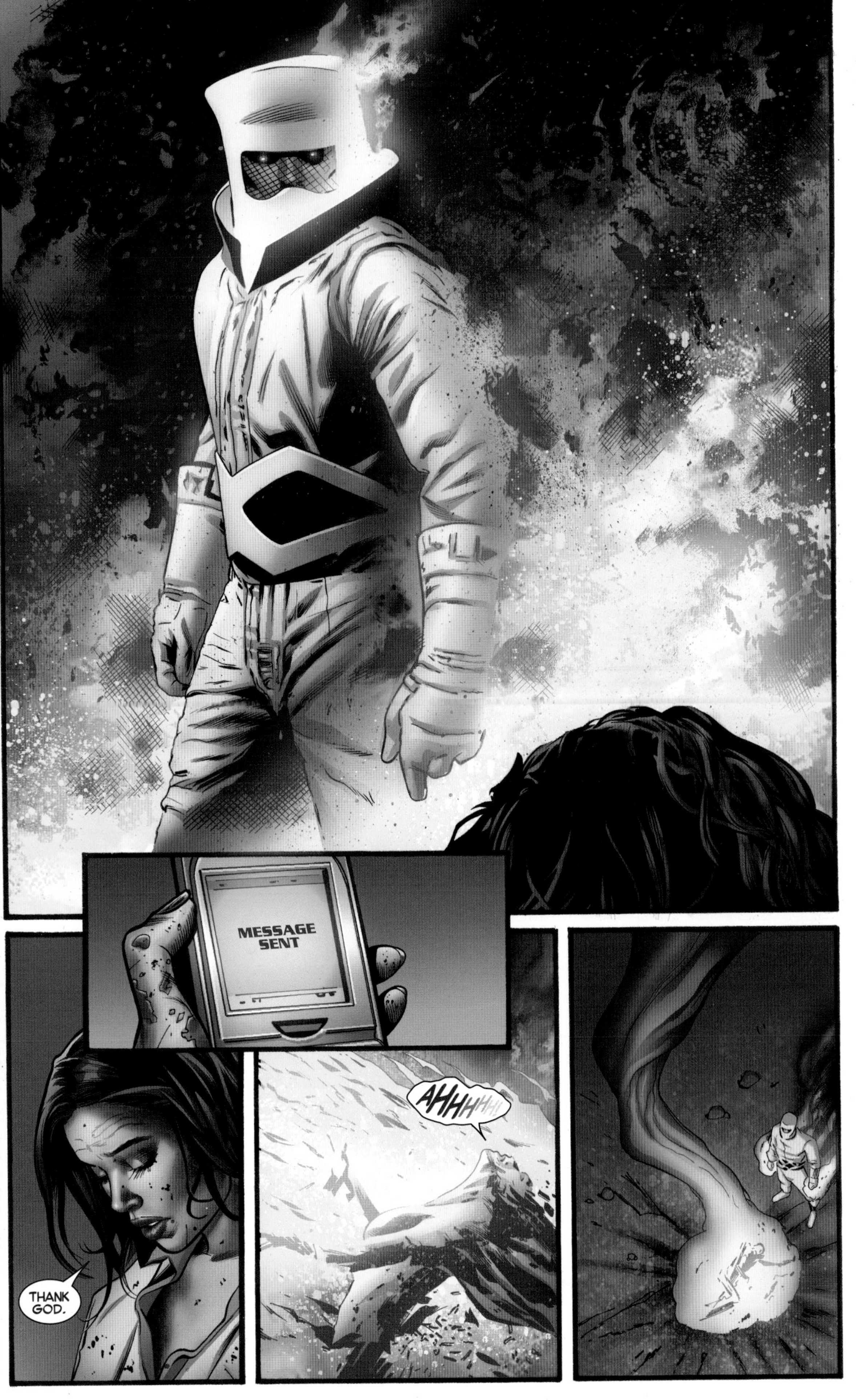
MESSAGE SENT
THANK GOD.
AHHHHH!

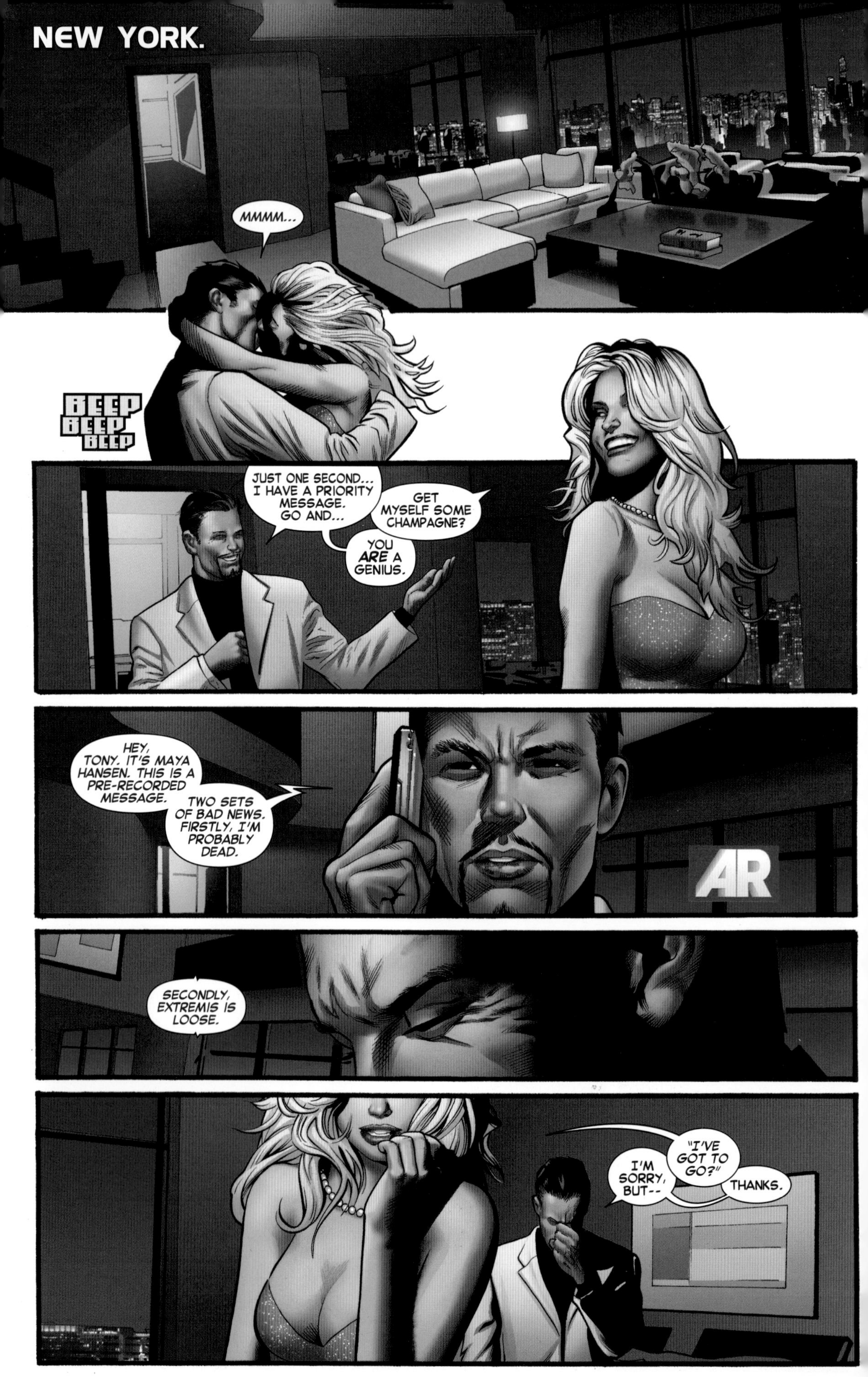
NEW YORK.
MMMM...
BEEP BEEP BEEP
JUST ONE SECOND... I HAVE A PRIORITY MESSAGE. GO AND...
GET MYSELF SOME CHAMPAGNE?
YOU ARE A GENIUS.
HEY, TONY. IT'S MAYA HANSEN. THIS IS A PRE-RECORDED MESSAGE.
TWO SETS OF BAD NEWS. FIRSTLY, I'M PROBABLY DEAD.
AR
SECONDLY, EXTREMIS IS LOOSE.
I'M SORRY, BUT--
"I'VE GOT TO GO?"
THANKS.

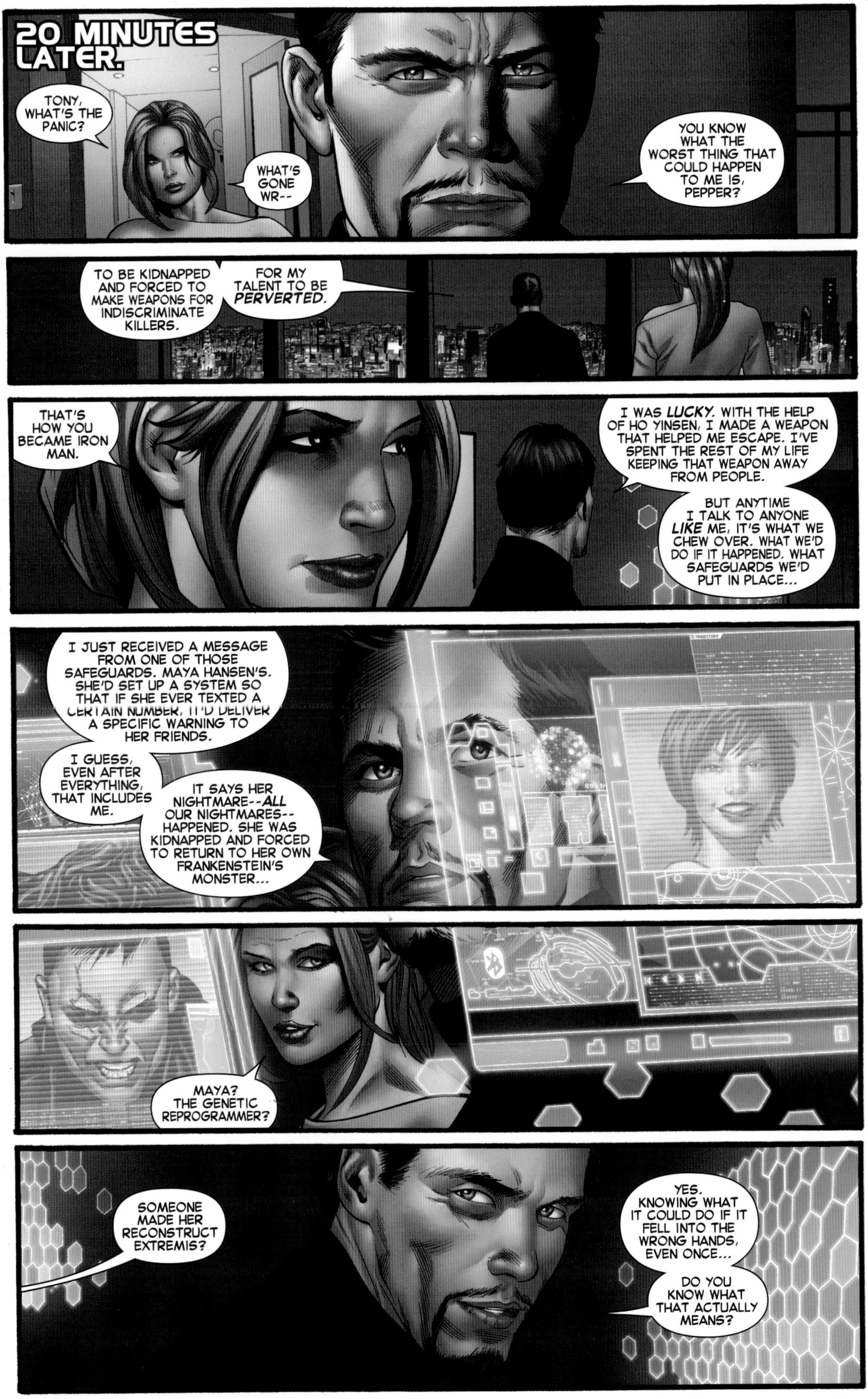
20 MINUTES LATER.
TONY, WHAT'S THE PANIC?
WHAT'S GONE WR--
YOU KNOW WHAT THE WORST THING THAT COULD HAPPEN TO ME IS, PEPPER?
TO BE KIDNAPPED AND FORCED TO MAKE WEAPONS FOR INDISCRIMINATE KILLERS.
FOR MY TALENT TO BE *PERVERTED*.
THAT'S HOW YOU BECAME IRON MAN.
I WAS *LUCKY*. WITH THE HELP OF HO YINSEN, I MADE A WEAPON THAT HELPED ME ESCAPE. I'VE SPENT THE REST OF MY LIFE KEEPING THAT WEAPON AWAY FROM PEOPLE.
BUT ANYTIME I TALK TO ANYONE *LIKE* ME, IT'S WHAT WE CHEW OVER. WHAT WE'D DO IF IT HAPPENED. WHAT SAFEGUARDS WE'D PUT IN PLACE...
I JUST RECEIVED A MESSAGE FROM ONE OF THOSE SAFEGUARDS. MAYA HANSEN'S. SHE'D SET UP A SYSTEM SO THAT IF SHE EVER TEXTED A CERTAIN NUMBER, IT'D DELIVER A SPECIFIC WARNING TO HER FRIENDS.
I GUESS, EVEN AFTER EVERYTHING, THAT INCLUDES ME.
IT SAYS HER NIGHTMARE--*ALL* OUR NIGHTMARES--HAPPENED. SHE WAS KIDNAPPED AND FORCED TO RETURN TO HER OWN FRANKENSTEIN'S MONSTER...
MAYA? THE GENETIC REPROGRAMMER?
SOMEONE MADE HER RECONSTRUCT EXTREMIS?
YES. KNOWING WHAT IT COULD DO IF IT FELL INTO THE WRONG HANDS, EVEN ONCE...
DO YOU KNOW WHAT THAT ACTUALLY MEANS?

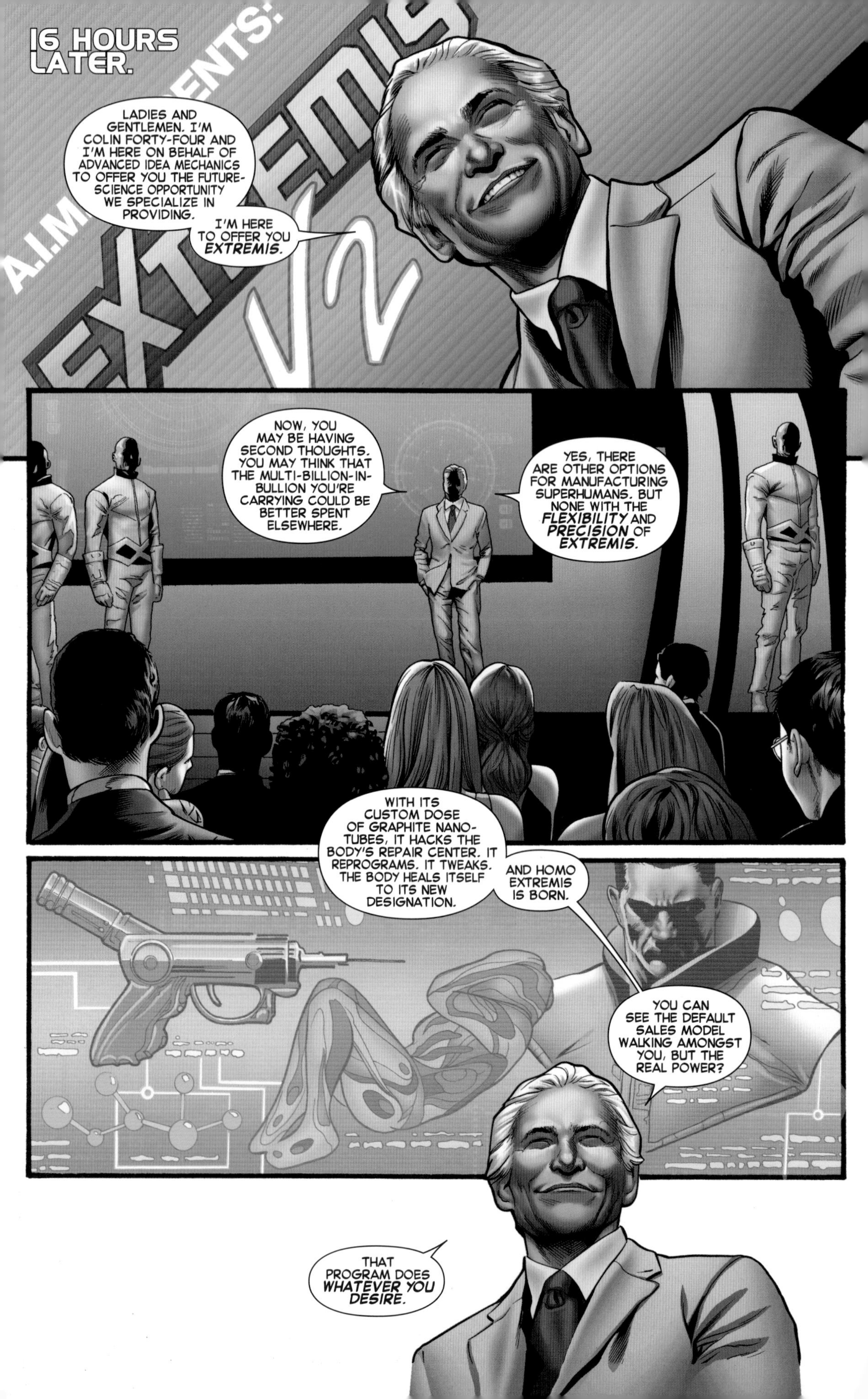
16 HOURS LATER.
A.I.M. PRESENTS: EXTREMIS V2
LADIES AND GENTLEMEN. I'M COLIN FORTY-FOUR AND I'M HERE ON BEHALF OF ADVANCED IDEA MECHANICS TO OFFER YOU THE FUTURE-SCIENCE OPPORTUNITY WE SPECIALIZE IN PROVIDING.
I'M HERE TO OFFER YOU EXTREMIS.
NOW, YOU MAY BE HAVING SECOND THOUGHTS. YOU MAY THINK THAT THE MULTI-BILLION-IN-BULLION YOU'RE CARRYING COULD BE BETTER SPENT ELSEWHERE.
YES, THERE ARE OTHER OPTIONS FOR MANUFACTURING SUPERHUMANS. BUT NONE WITH THE FLEXIBILITY AND PRECISION OF EXTREMIS.
WITH ITS CUSTOM DOSE OF GRAPHITE NANO-TUBES, IT HACKS THE BODY'S REPAIR CENTER. IT REPROGRAMS. IT TWEAKS. THE BODY HEALS ITSELF TO ITS NEW DESIGNATION.
AND HOMO EXTREMIS IS BORN.
YOU CAN SEE THE DEFAULT SALES MODEL WALKING AMONGST YOU, BUT THE REAL POWER?
THAT PROGRAM DOES WHATEVER YOU DESIRE.

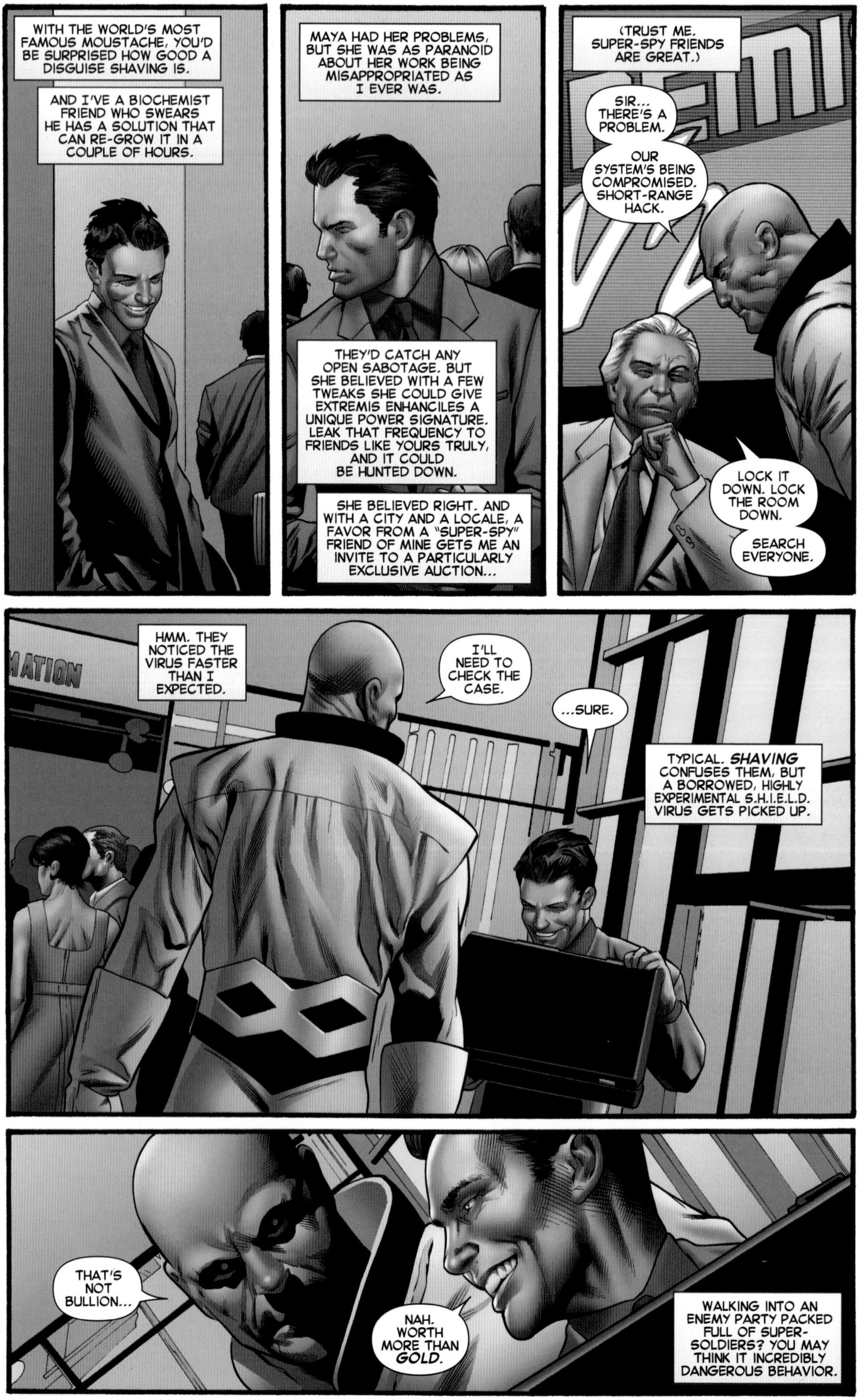
WITH THE WORLD'S MOST FAMOUS MOUSTACHE, YOU'D BE SURPRISED HOW GOOD A DISGUISE SHAVING IS.
AND I'VE A BIOCHEMIST FRIEND WHO SWEARS HE HAS A SOLUTION THAT CAN RE-GROW IT IN A COUPLE OF HOURS.
MAYA HAD HER PROBLEMS, BUT SHE WAS AS PARANOID ABOUT HER WORK BEING MISAPPROPRIATED AS I EVER WAS.
THEY'D CATCH ANY OPEN SABOTAGE. BUT SHE BELIEVED WITH A FEW TWEAKS SHE COULD GIVE EXTREMIS ENHANCILES A UNIQUE POWER SIGNATURE. LEAK THAT FREQUENCY TO FRIENDS LIKE YOURS TRULY, AND IT COULD BE HUNTED DOWN.
SHE BELIEVED RIGHT. AND WITH A CITY AND A LOCALE, A FAVOR FROM A "SUPER-SPY" FRIEND OF MINE GETS ME AN INVITE TO A PARTICULARLY EXCLUSIVE AUCTION...
(TRUST ME. SUPER-SPY FRIENDS ARE GREAT.)
SIR... THERE'S A PROBLEM.
OUR SYSTEM'S BEING COMPROMISED. SHORT-RANGE HACK.
LOCK IT DOWN. LOCK THE ROOM DOWN.
SEARCH EVERYONE.
HMM. THEY NOTICED THE VIRUS FASTER THAN I EXPECTED.
I'LL NEED TO CHECK THE CASE.
...SURE.
TYPICAL. SHAVING CONFUSES THEM, BUT A BORROWED, HIGHLY EXPERIMENTAL S.H.I.E.L.D. VIRUS GETS PICKED UP.
THAT'S NOT BULLION...
NAH. WORTH MORE THAN GOLD.
WALKING INTO AN ENEMY PARTY PACKED FULL OF SUPER-SOLDIERS? YOU MAY THINK IT INCREDIBLY DANGEROUS BEHAVIOR.

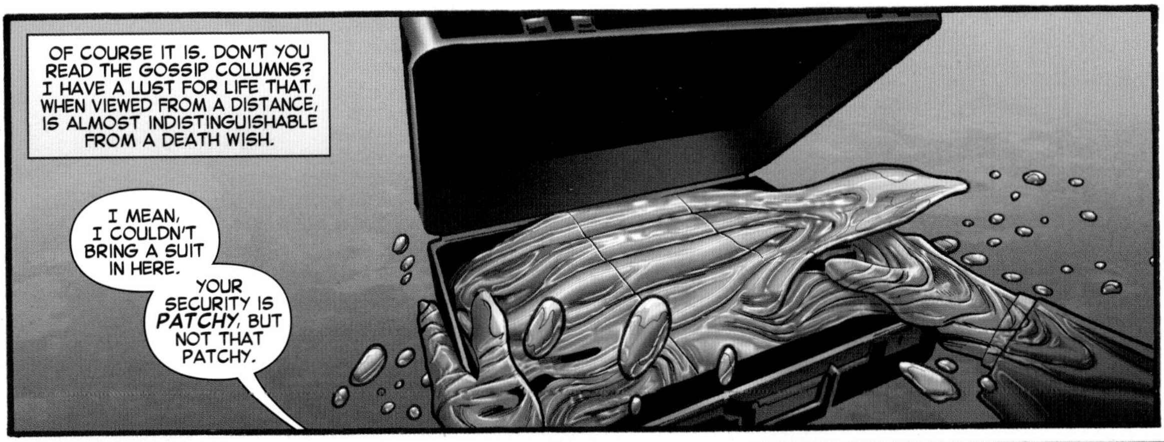
OF COURSE IT IS. DON'T YOU READ THE GOSSIP COLUMNS? I HAVE A LUST FOR LIFE THAT, WHEN VIEWED FROM A DISTANCE, IS ALMOST INDISTINGUISHABLE FROM A DEATH WISH.
I MEAN, I COULDN'T BRING A SUIT IN HERE.
YOUR SECURITY IS *PATCHY*, BUT NOT THAT PATCHY.

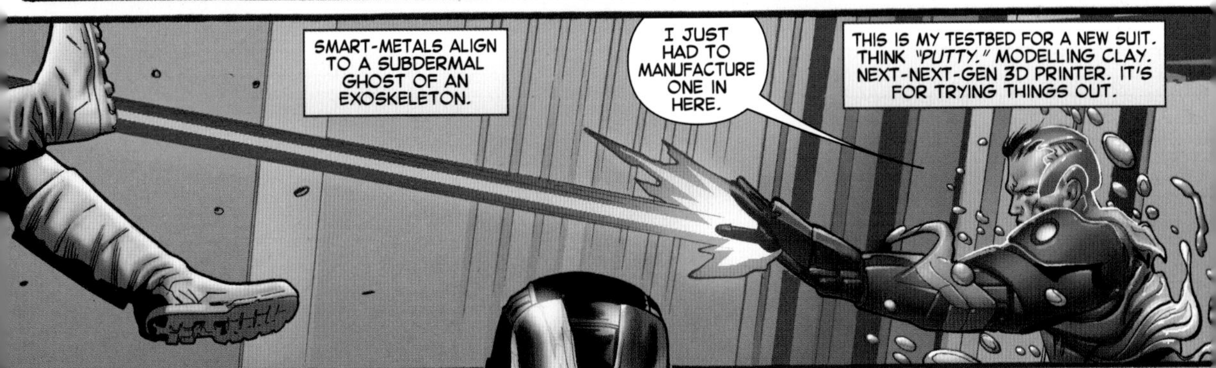
SMART-METALS ALIGN TO A SUBDERMAL GHOST OF AN EXOSKELETON.
I JUST HAD TO MANUFACTURE ONE IN HERE.
THIS IS MY TESTBED FOR A NEW SUIT. THINK "PUTTY." MODELLING CLAY. NEXT-NEXT-GEN 3D PRINTER. IT'S FOR TRYING THINGS OUT.

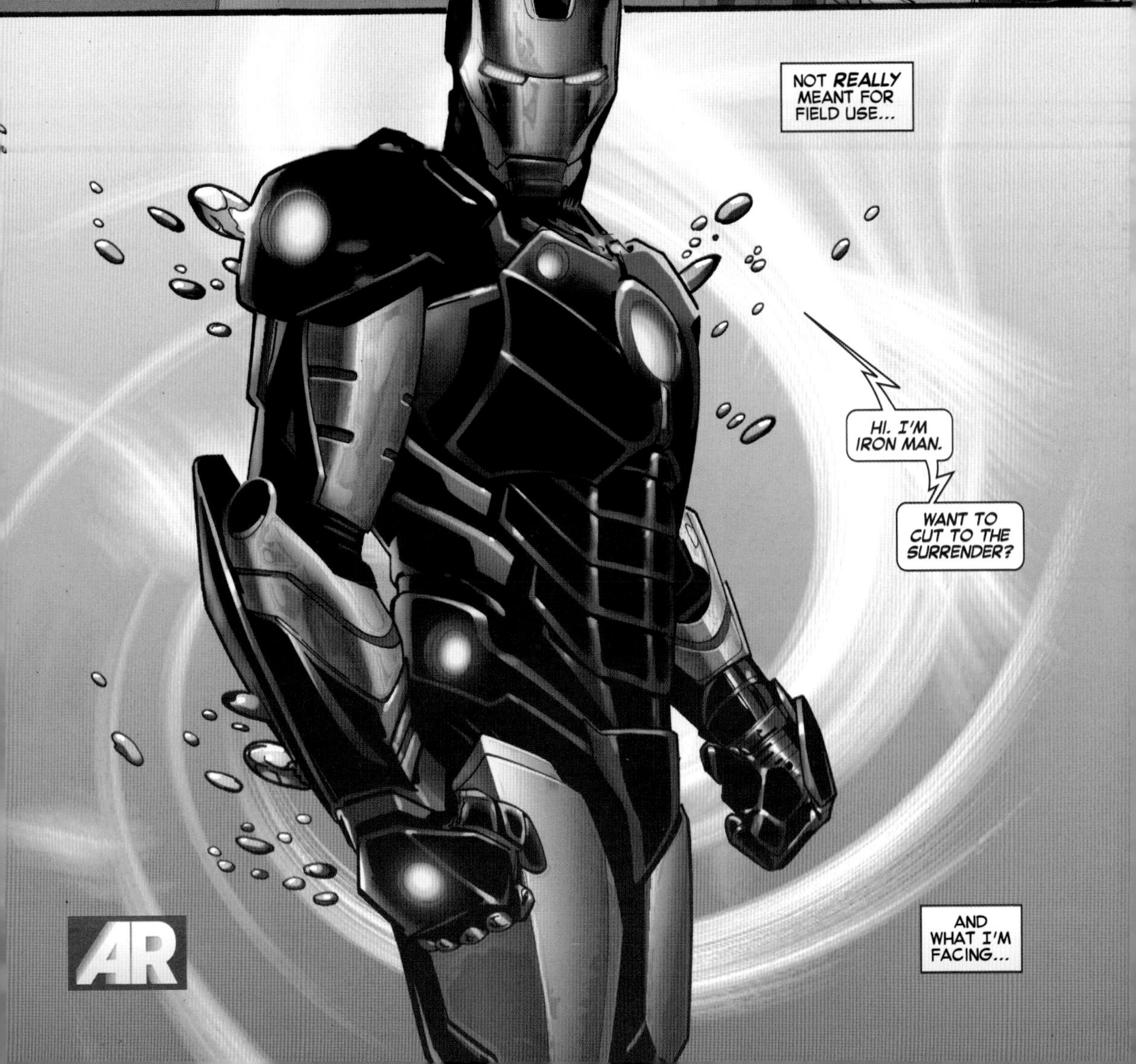
NOT *REALLY* MEANT FOR FIELD USE...
HI. I'M IRON MAN.
WANT TO CUT TO THE SURRENDER?
AND WHAT I'M FACING...

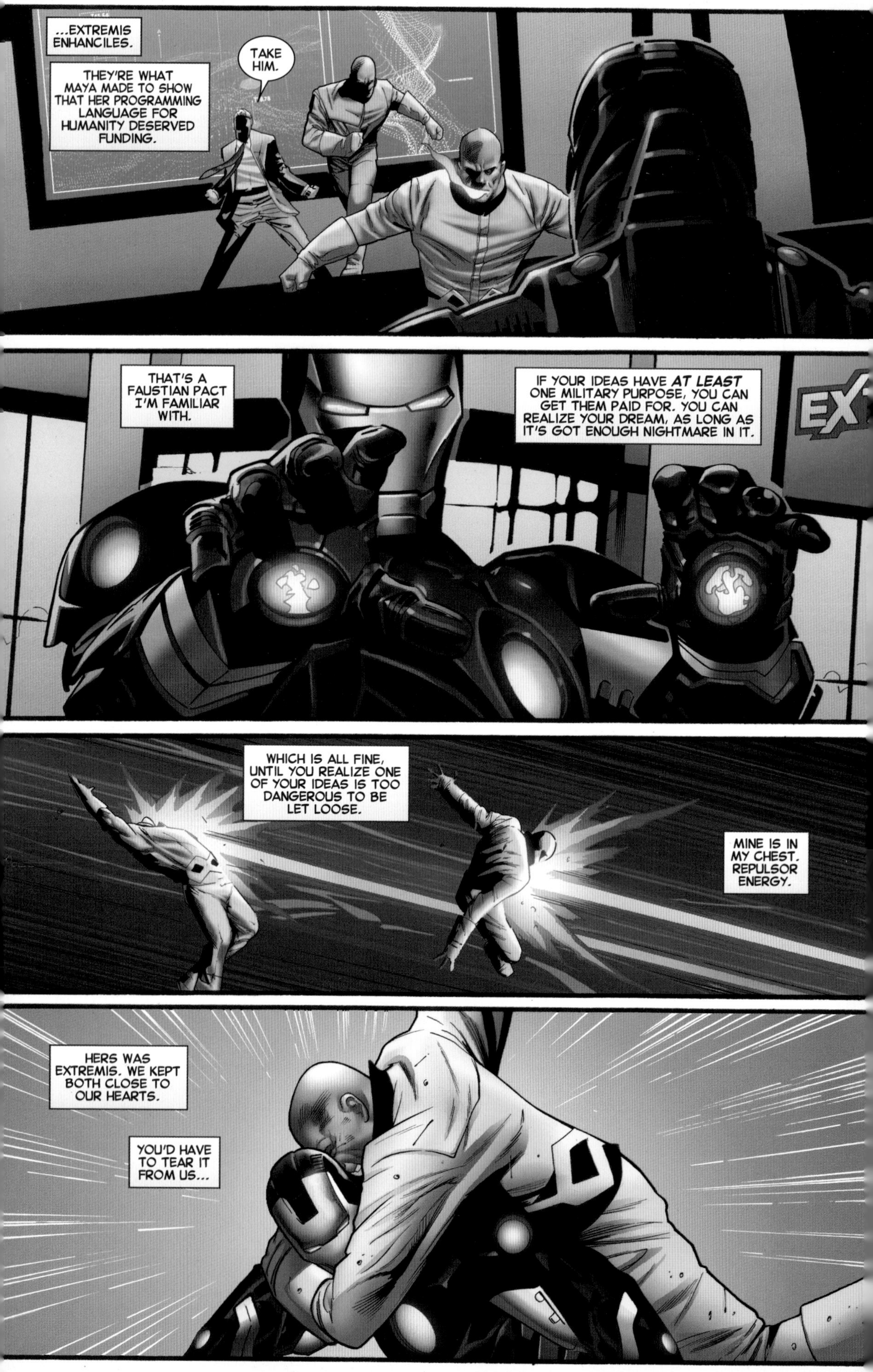
...EXTREMIS ENHANCILES.
THEY'RE WHAT MAYA MADE TO SHOW THAT HER PROGRAMMING LANGUAGE FOR HUMANITY DESERVED FUNDING.
TAKE HIM.
THAT'S A FAUSTIAN PACT I'M FAMILIAR WITH.
IF YOUR IDEAS HAVE *AT LEAST* ONE MILITARY PURPOSE, YOU CAN GET THEM PAID FOR. YOU CAN REALIZE YOUR DREAM, AS LONG AS IT'S GOT ENOUGH NIGHTMARE IN IT.
WHICH IS ALL FINE, UNTIL YOU REALIZE ONE OF YOUR IDEAS IS TOO DANGEROUS TO BE LET LOOSE.
MINE IS IN MY CHEST. REPULSOR ENERGY.
HERS WAS EXTREMIS. WE KEPT BOTH CLOSE TO OUR HEARTS.
YOU'D HAVE TO TEAR IT FROM US...

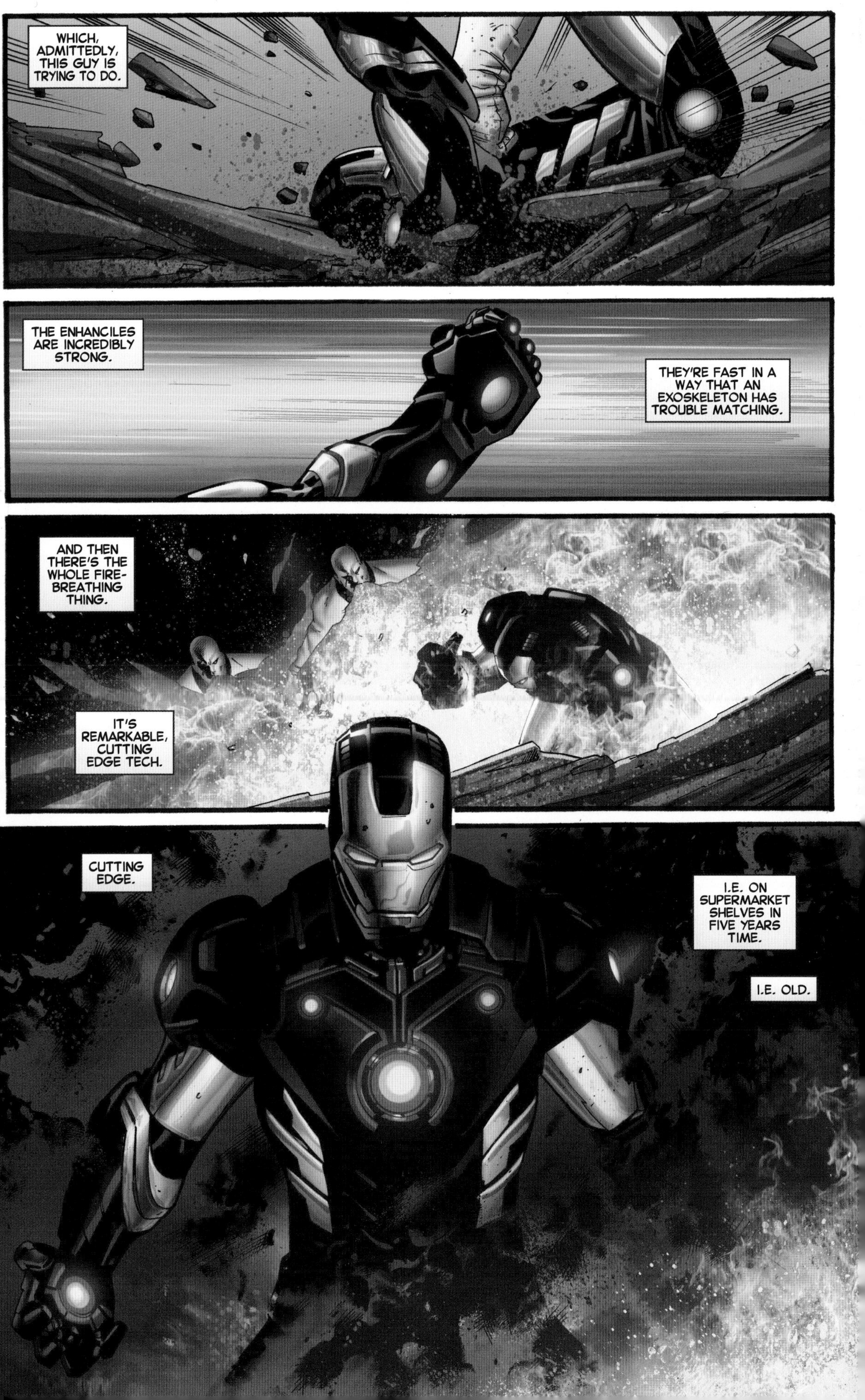
WHICH, ADMITTEDLY, THIS GUY IS TRYING TO DO.
THE ENHANCILES ARE INCREDIBLY STRONG.
THEY'RE FAST IN A WAY THAT AN EXOSKELETON HAS TROUBLE MATCHING.
AND THEN THERE'S THE WHOLE FIRE-BREATHING THING.
IT'S REMARKABLE, CUTTING EDGE TECH.
CUTTING EDGE.
I.E. ON SUPERMARKET SHELVES IN FIVE YEARS TIME.
I.E. OLD.

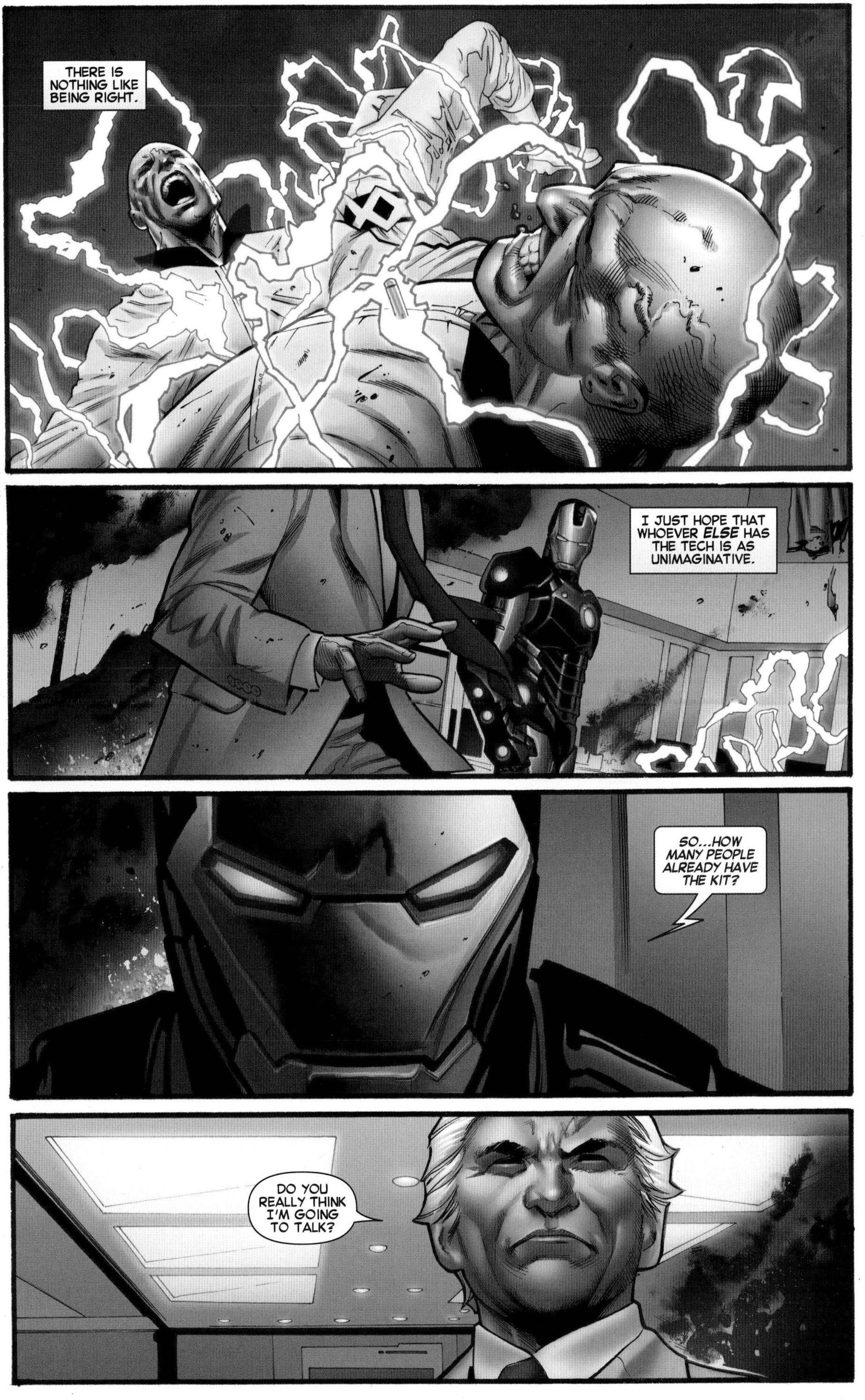
THERE IS NOTHING LIKE BEING RIGHT.
I JUST HOPE THAT WHOEVER ELSE HAS THE TECH IS AS UNIMAGINATIVE.
SO...HOW MANY PEOPLE ALREADY HAVE THE KIT?
DO YOU REALLY THINK I'M GOING TO TALK?

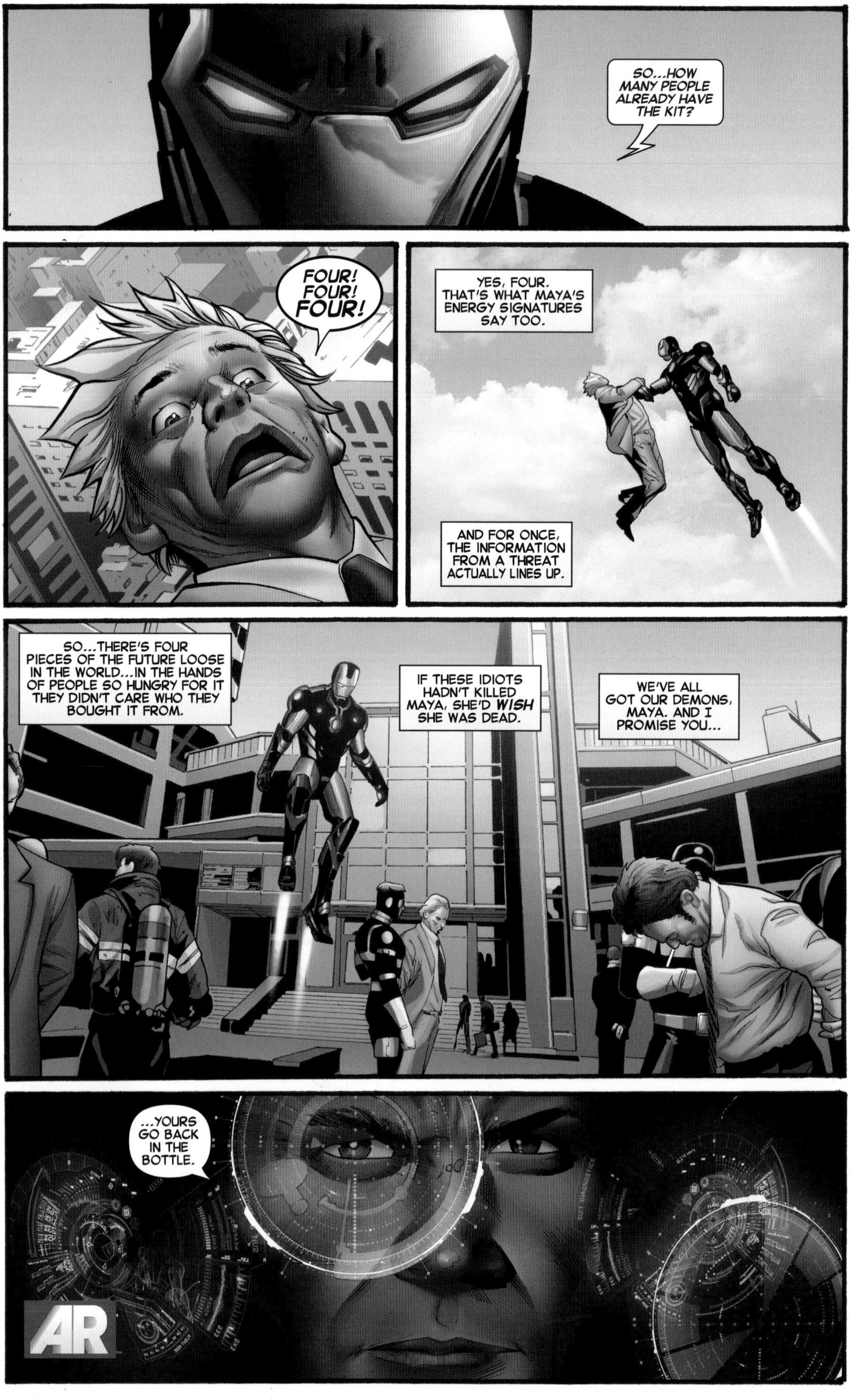
SO...HOW MANY PEOPLE ALREADY HAVE THE KIT?
FOUR! FOUR! FOUR!
YES, FOUR. THAT'S WHAT MAYA'S ENERGY SIGNATURES SAY TOO.
AND FOR ONCE, THE INFORMATION FROM A THREAT ACTUALLY LINES UP.
SO...THERE'S FOUR PIECES OF THE FUTURE LOOSE IN THE WORLD...IN THE HANDS OF PEOPLE SO HUNGRY FOR IT THEY DIDN'T CARE WHO THEY BOUGHT IT FROM.
IF THESE IDIOTS HADN'T KILLED MAYA, SHE'D WISH SHE WAS DEAD.
WE'VE ALL GOT OUR DEMONS, MAYA. AND I PROMISE YOU...
...YOURS GO BACK IN THE BOTTLE.
AR

MARVEL GRAPHIC NOVEL

IRON MAN #2

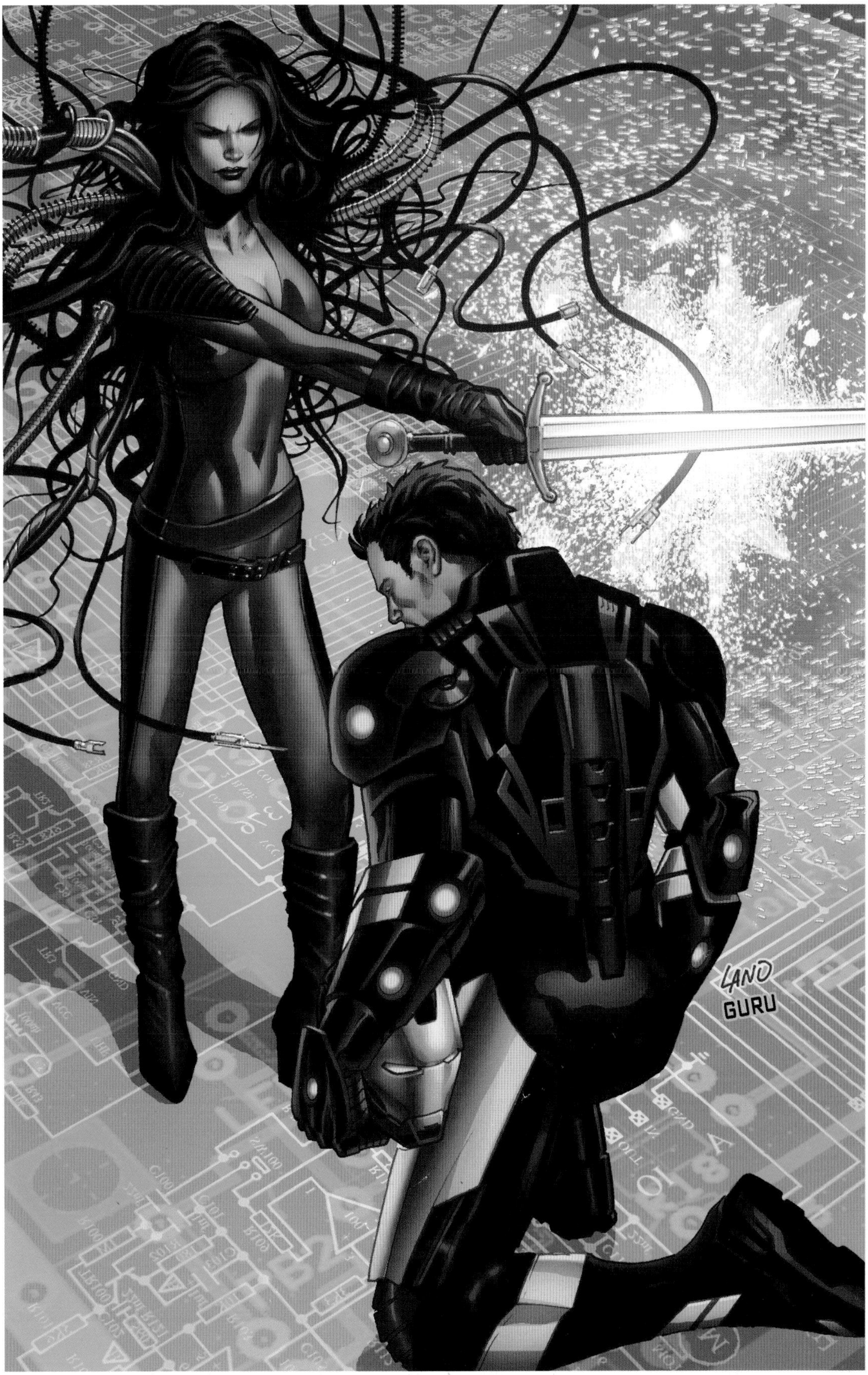
LAND
GURU

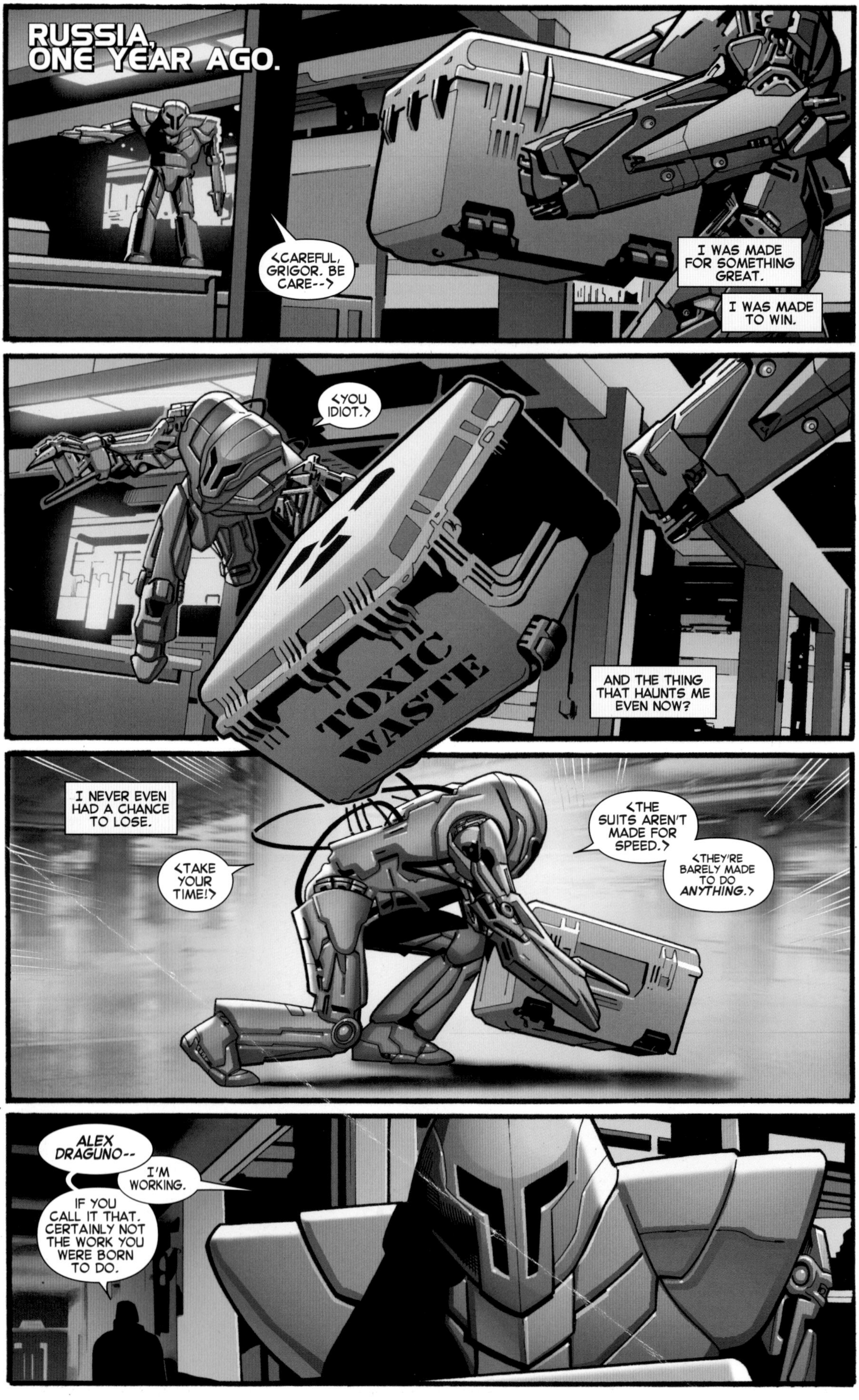
RUSSIA, ONE YEAR AGO.
<CAREFUL, GRIGOR. BE CARE-->
I WAS MADE FOR SOMETHING GREAT.
I WAS MADE TO WIN.
<YOU IDIOT.>
TOXIC WASTE
AND THE THING THAT HAUNTS ME EVEN NOW?
I NEVER EVEN HAD A CHANCE TO LOSE.
<TAKE YOUR TIME!>
<THE SUITS AREN'T MADE FOR SPEED.>
<THEY'RE BARELY MADE TO DO ANYTHING.>
ALEX DRAGUNO--
I'M WORKING.
IF YOU CALL IT THAT. CERTAINLY NOT THE WORK YOU WERE BORN TO DO.

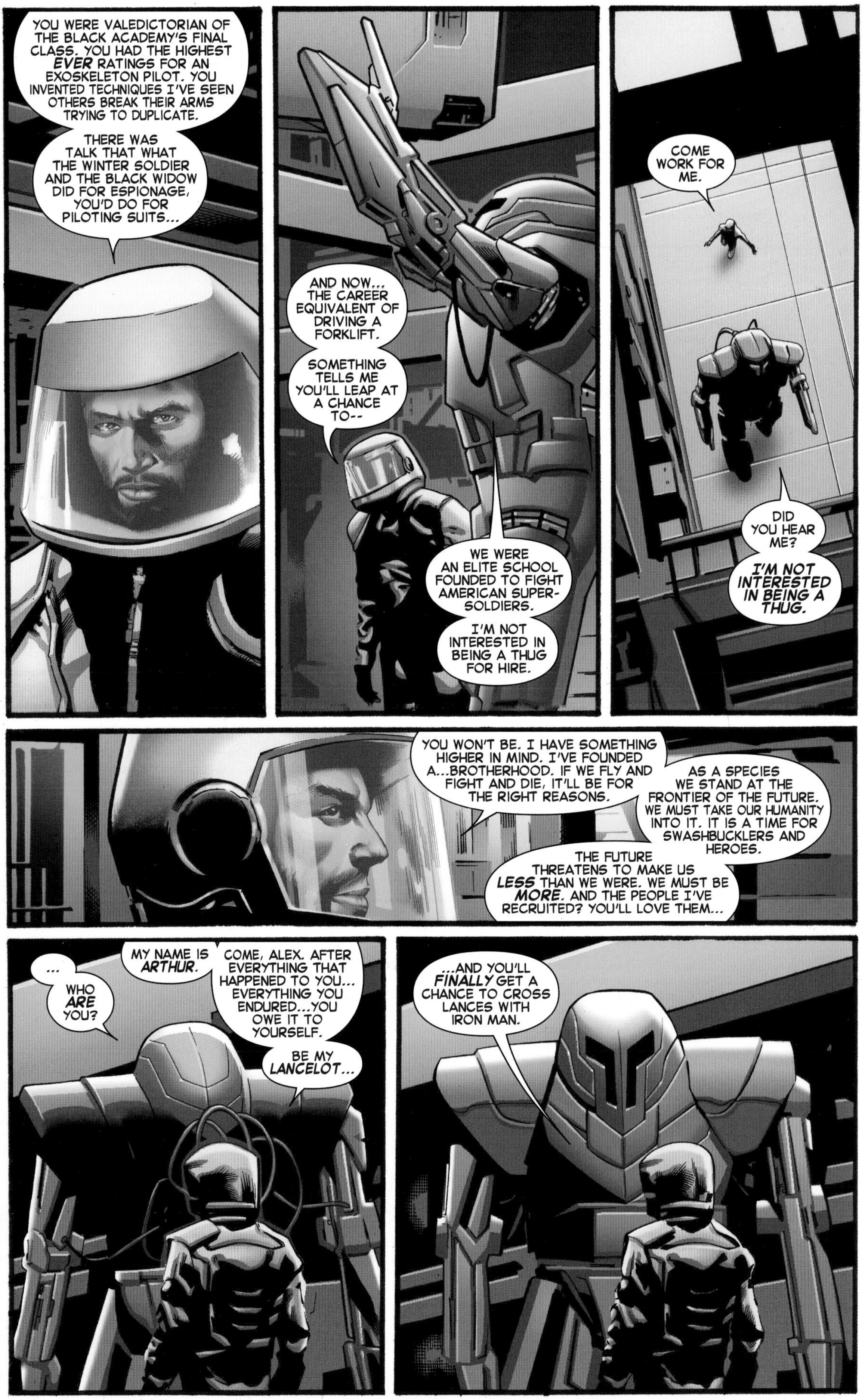
YOU WERE VALEDICTORIAN OF THE BLACK ACADEMY'S FINAL CLASS. YOU HAD THE HIGHEST EVER RATINGS FOR AN EXOSKELETON PILOT. YOU INVENTED TECHNIQUES I'VE SEEN OTHERS BREAK THEIR ARMS TRYING TO DUPLICATE.
THERE WAS TALK THAT WHAT THE WINTER SOLDIER AND THE BLACK WIDOW DID FOR ESPIONAGE, YOU'D DO FOR PILOTING SUITS...
AND NOW... THE CAREER EQUIVALENT OF DRIVING A FORKLIFT.
SOMETHING TELLS ME YOU'LL LEAP AT A CHANCE TO--
WE WERE AN ELITE SCHOOL FOUNDED TO FIGHT AMERICAN SUPER-SOLDIERS.
I'M NOT INTERESTED IN BEING A THUG FOR HIRE.
COME WORK FOR ME.
DID YOU HEAR ME?
I'M NOT INTERESTED IN BEING A THUG.
YOU WON'T BE. I HAVE SOMETHING HIGHER IN MIND. I'VE FOUNDED A...BROTHERHOOD. IF WE FLY AND FIGHT AND DIE, IT'LL BE FOR THE RIGHT REASONS.
AS A SPECIES WE STAND AT THE FRONTIER OF THE FUTURE. WE MUST TAKE OUR HUMANITY INTO IT. IT IS A TIME FOR SWASHBUCKLERS AND HEROES.
THE FUTURE THREATENS TO MAKE US LESS THAN WE WERE. WE MUST BE MORE. AND THE PEOPLE I'VE RECRUITED? YOU'LL LOVE THEM...
... WHO ARE YOU?
MY NAME IS ARTHUR.
COME, ALEX. AFTER EVERYTHING THAT HAPPENED TO YOU... EVERYTHING YOU ENDURED...YOU OWE IT TO YOURSELF.
BE MY LANCELOT...
...AND YOU'LL FINALLY GET A CHANCE TO CROSS LANCES WITH IRON MAN.

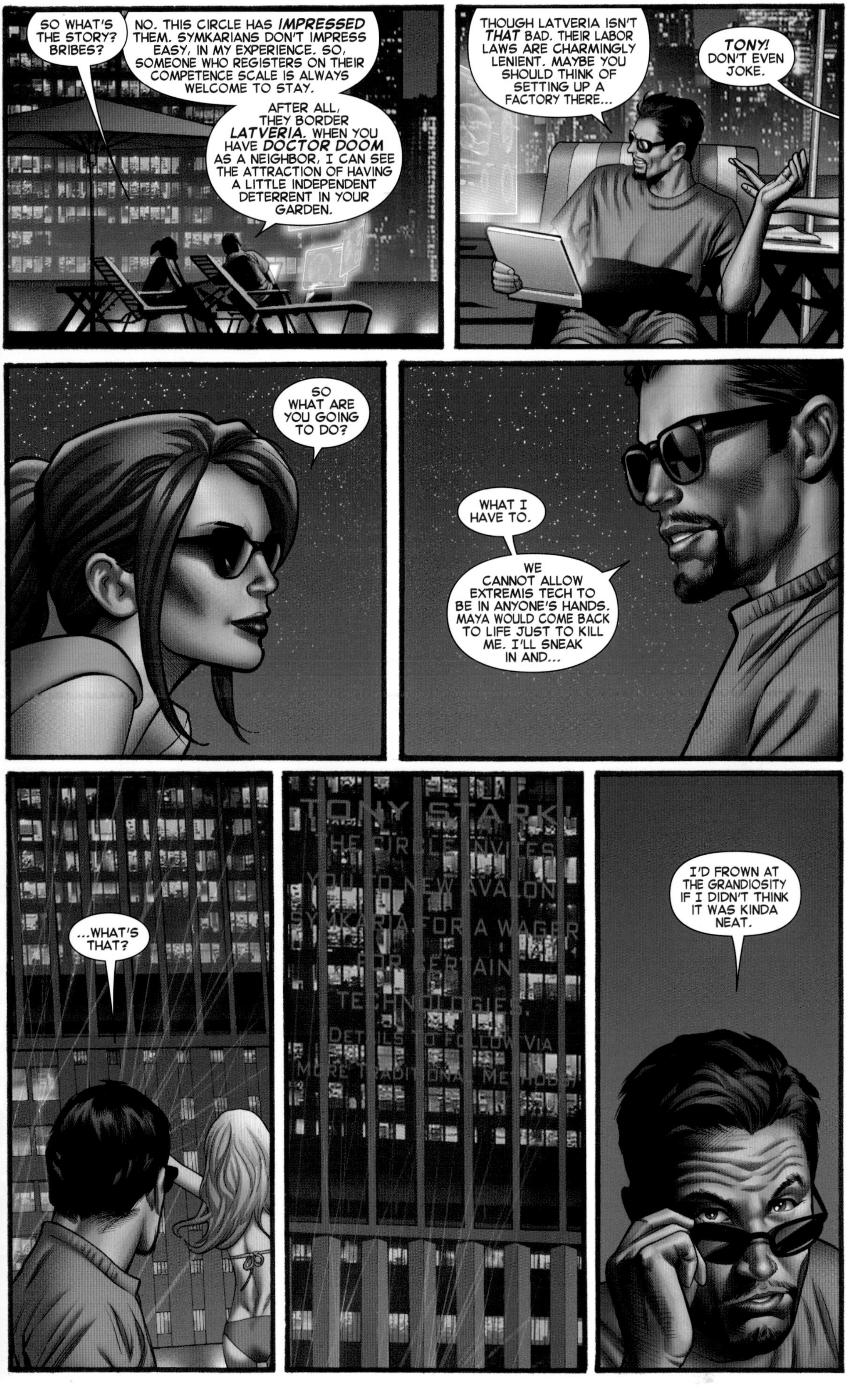

SO WHAT'S THE STORY? BRIBES?
NO. THIS CIRCLE HAS *IMPRESSED* THEM. SYMKARIANS DON'T IMPRESS EASY, IN MY EXPERIENCE. SO, SOMEONE WHO REGISTERS ON THEIR COMPETENCE SCALE IS ALWAYS WELCOME TO STAY.
AFTER ALL, THEY BORDER *LATVERIA.* WHEN YOU HAVE *DOCTOR DOOM* AS A NEIGHBOR, I CAN SEE THE ATTRACTION OF HAVING A LITTLE INDEPENDENT DETERRENT IN YOUR GARDEN.
THOUGH LATVERIA ISN'T *THAT* BAD. THEIR LABOR LAWS ARE CHARMINGLY LENIENT. MAYBE YOU SHOULD THINK OF SETTING UP A FACTORY THERE...
TONY! DON'T EVEN JOKE.
SO WHAT ARE YOU GOING TO DO?
WHAT I HAVE TO.
WE CANNOT ALLOW EXTREMIS TECH TO BE IN ANYONE'S HANDS. MAYA WOULD COME BACK TO LIFE JUST TO KILL ME. I'LL SNEAK IN AND...
...WHAT'S THAT?
TONY STARK!
THE CIRCLE INVITES
YOU TO NEW AVALON,
SYMKARIA FOR A WAGER
FOR CERTAIN
TECHNOLOGIES.
DETAILS TO FOLLOW VIA
MORE TRADITIONAL METHODS.
I'D FROWN AT THE GRANDIOSITY IF I DIDN'T THINK IT WAS KINDA NEAT.

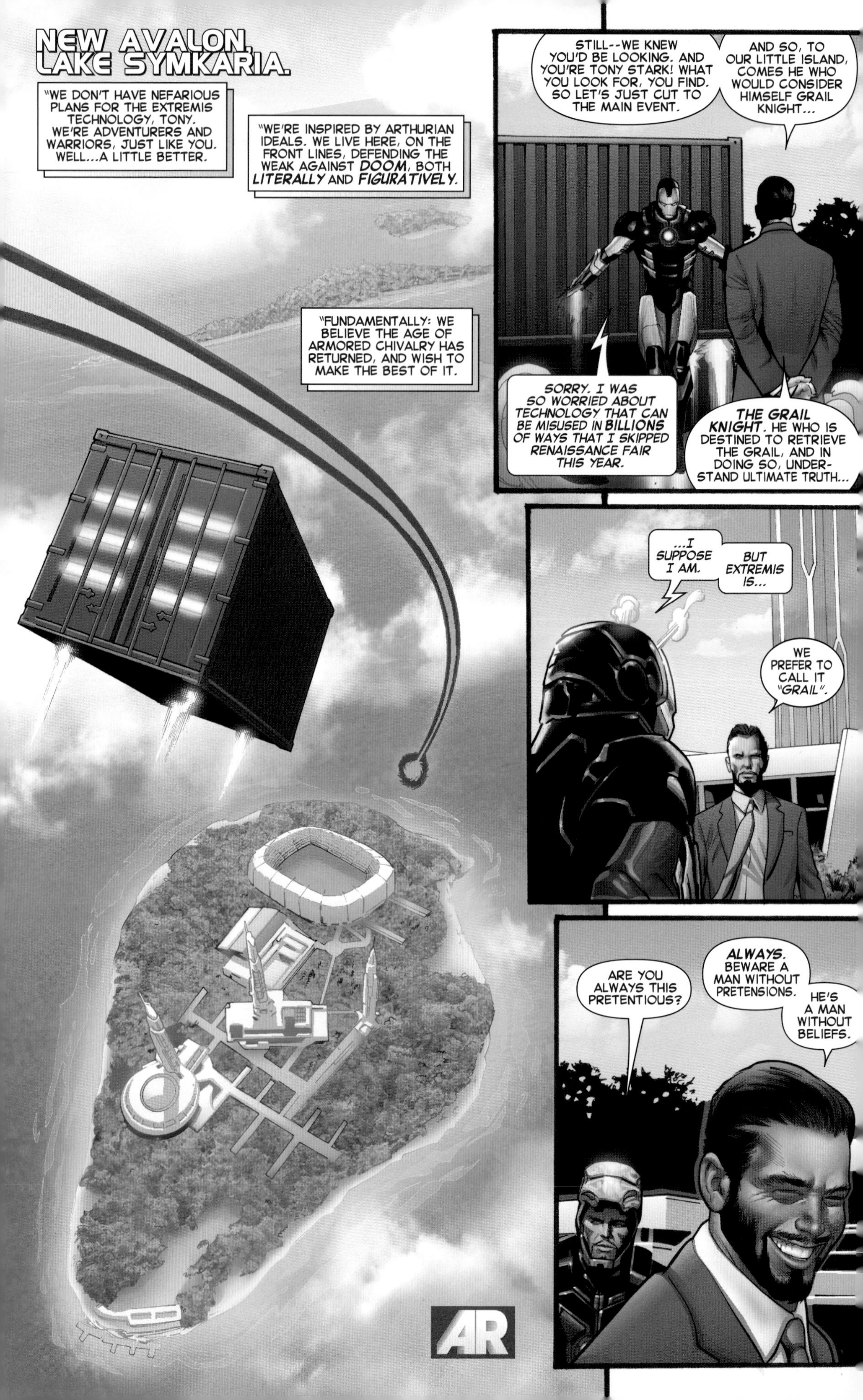
NEW AVALON, LAKE SYMKARIA.
"WE DON'T HAVE NEFARIOUS PLANS FOR THE EXTREMIS TECHNOLOGY, TONY. WE'RE ADVENTURERS AND WARRIORS, JUST LIKE YOU. WELL...A LITTLE BETTER.
"WE'RE INSPIRED BY ARTHURIAN IDEALS. WE LIVE HERE, ON THE FRONT LINES, DEFENDING THE WEAK AGAINST DOOM, BOTH LITERALLY AND FIGURATIVELY.
"FUNDAMENTALLY: WE BELIEVE THE AGE OF ARMORED CHIVALRY HAS RETURNED, AND WISH TO MAKE THE BEST OF IT.
STILL--WE KNEW YOU'D BE LOOKING. AND YOU'RE TONY STARK! WHAT YOU LOOK FOR, YOU FIND. SO LET'S JUST CUT TO THE MAIN EVENT.
AND SO, TO OUR LITTLE ISLAND, COMES HE WHO WOULD CONSIDER HIMSELF GRAIL KNIGHT...
SORRY. I WAS SO WORRIED ABOUT TECHNOLOGY THAT CAN BE MISUSED IN BILLIONS OF WAYS THAT I SKIPPED RENAISSANCE FAIR THIS YEAR.
THE GRAIL KNIGHT. HE WHO IS DESTINED TO RETRIEVE THE GRAIL, AND IN DOING SO, UNDERSTAND ULTIMATE TRUTH...
...I SUPPOSE I AM.
BUT EXTREMIS IS...
WE PREFER TO CALL IT "GRAIL".
ARE YOU ALWAYS THIS PRETENTIOUS?
ALWAYS. BEWARE A MAN WITHOUT PRETENSIONS.
HE'S A MAN WITHOUT BELIEFS.
AR

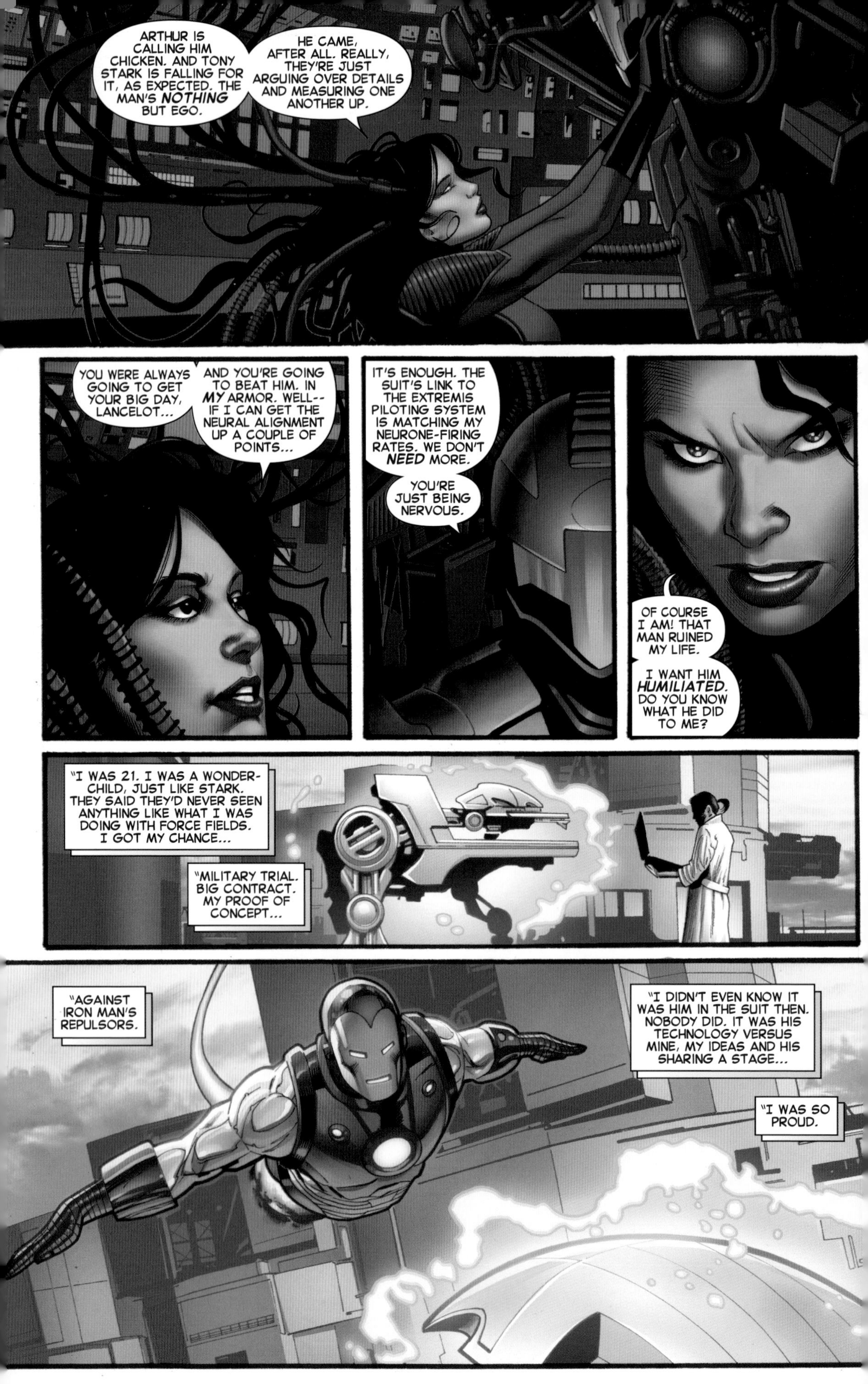
ARTHUR IS CALLING HIM CHICKEN. AND TONY STARK IS FALLING FOR IT, AS EXPECTED. THE MAN'S NOTHING BUT EGO.
HE CAME, AFTER ALL. REALLY, THEY'RE JUST ARGUING OVER DETAILS AND MEASURING ONE ANOTHER UP.
YOU WERE ALWAYS GOING TO GET YOUR BIG DAY, LANCELOT...
AND YOU'RE GOING TO BEAT HIM. IN MY ARMOR. WELL-- IF I CAN GET THE NEURAL ALIGNMENT UP A COUPLE OF POINTS...
IT'S ENOUGH. THE SUIT'S LINK TO THE EXTREMIS PILOTING SYSTEM IS MATCHING MY NEURONE-FIRING RATES. WE DON'T NEED MORE.
YOU'RE JUST BEING NERVOUS.
OF COURSE I AM! THAT MAN RUINED MY LIFE.
I WANT HIM HUMILIATED. DO YOU KNOW WHAT HE DID TO ME?
"I WAS 21. I WAS A WONDER-CHILD, JUST LIKE STARK. THEY SAID THEY'D NEVER SEEN ANYTHING LIKE WHAT I WAS DOING WITH FORCE FIELDS. I GOT MY CHANCE...
"MILITARY TRIAL. BIG CONTRACT. MY PROOF OF CONCEPT...
"AGAINST IRON MAN'S REPULSORS.
"I DIDN'T EVEN KNOW IT WAS HIM IN THE SUIT THEN. NOBODY DID. IT WAS HIS TECHNOLOGY VERSUS MINE, MY IDEAS AND HIS SHARING A STAGE...
"I WAS SO PROUD.

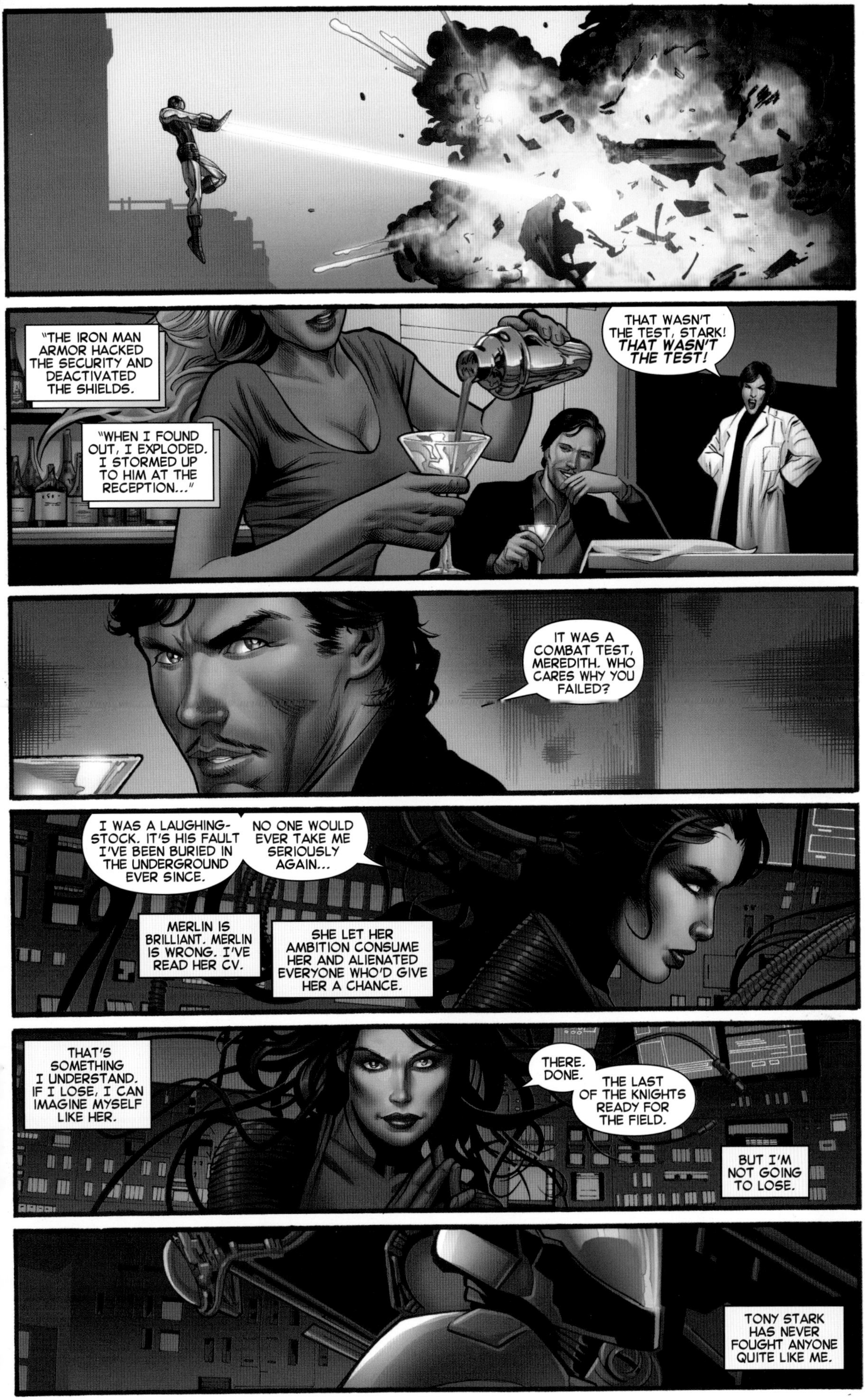
"THE IRON MAN ARMOR HACKED THE SECURITY AND DEACTIVATED THE SHIELDS.
"WHEN I FOUND OUT, I EXPLODED. I STORMED UP TO HIM AT THE RECEPTION..."
THAT WASN'T THE TEST, STARK! *THAT WASN'T THE TEST!*
IT WAS A COMBAT TEST, MEREDITH. WHO CARES WHY YOU FAILED?
I WAS A LAUGHING-STOCK. IT'S HIS FAULT I'VE BEEN BURIED IN THE UNDERGROUND EVER SINCE.
NO ONE WOULD EVER TAKE ME SERIOUSLY AGAIN...
MERLIN IS BRILLIANT. MERLIN IS WRONG. I'VE READ HER CV.
SHE LET HER AMBITION CONSUME HER AND ALIENATED EVERYONE WHO'D GIVE HER A CHANCE.
THAT'S SOMETHING I UNDERSTAND. IF I LOSE, I CAN IMAGINE MYSELF LIKE HER.
THERE. DONE.
THE LAST OF THE KNIGHTS READY FOR THE FIELD.
BUT I'M NOT GOING TO LOSE.
TONY STARK HAS NEVER FOUGHT ANYONE QUITE LIKE ME.

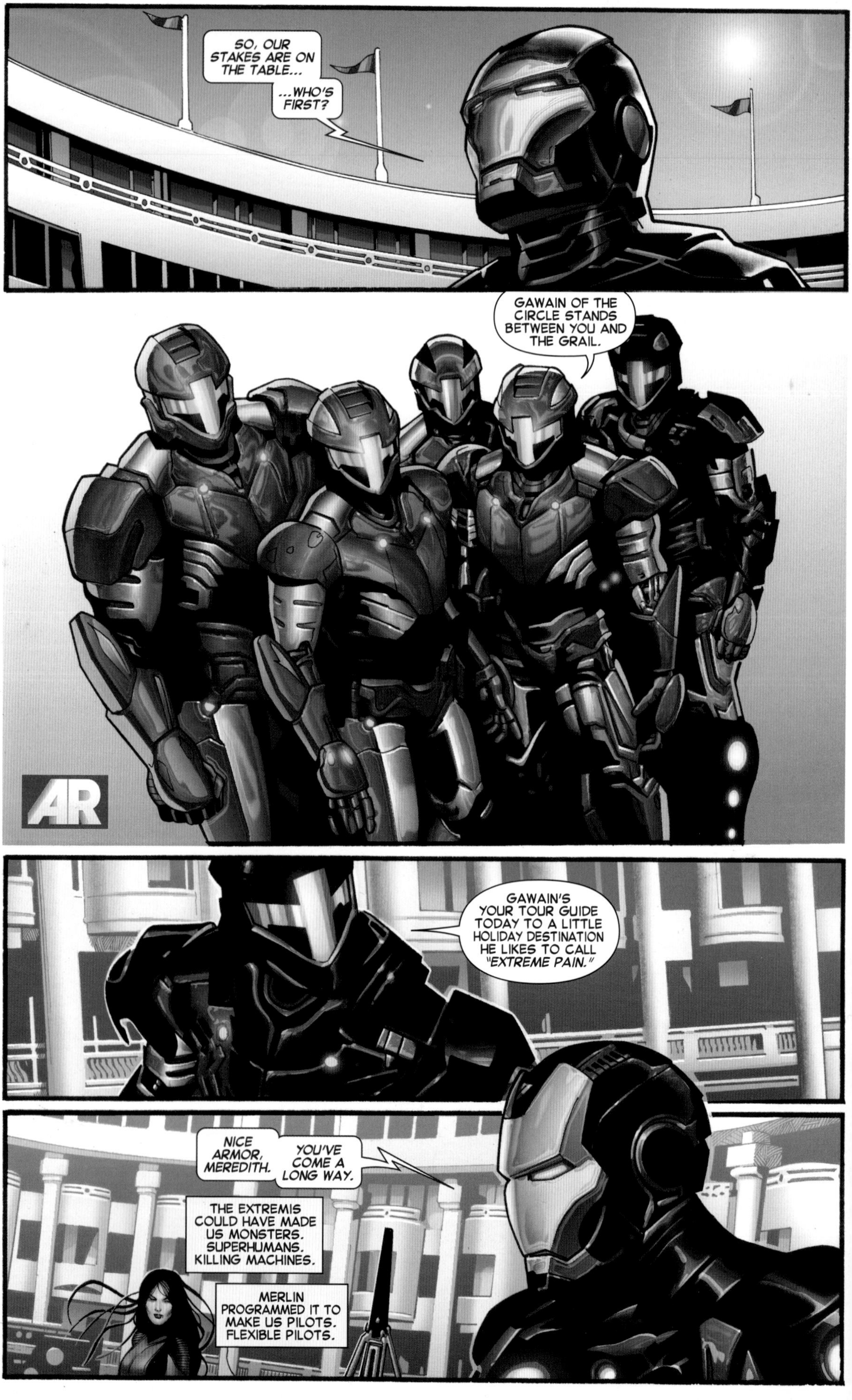

SO, OUR STAKES ARE ON THE TABLE...
...WHO'S FIRST?
GAWAIN OF THE CIRCLE STANDS BETWEEN YOU AND THE GRAIL.
GAWAIN'S YOUR TOUR GUIDE TODAY TO A LITTLE HOLIDAY DESTINATION HE LIKES TO CALL "EXTREME PAIN."
NICE ARMOR, MEREDITH.
YOU'VE COME A LONG WAY.
THE EXTREMIS COULD HAVE MADE US MONSTERS. SUPERHUMANS. KILLING MACHINES.
MERLIN PROGRAMMED IT TO MAKE US PILOTS. FLEXIBLE PILOTS.

WE ARE NOW LIVING CONTROL SYSTEMS, DIRECTLY CONNECTED TO WHATEVER SUITS MERLIN BUILDS. IT'S FUTURE-PROOFED. THE SUITS CAN IMPROVE WHILE THE PILOTS ARE AS GOOD AS THEY CAN GET WHILE STILL REMAINING HUMANS.

WELL, MOSTLY HUMAN. SOME MINOR BOOSTS. G-TOLERANCE AND SO ON, BUT THEY'RE NOT THE SORT OF THINGS THAT GET YOU INTO THE AVENGERS.

COMPUTER?

YZZ?

DEPLOY THE ARMORY.

YZZ!

GIVE ME A SINGLE-OPPONENT LOAD-OUT.

THROW THE LATEST REPULSOR IN THERE. THE MARK IVa.

IT'S ABOUT FLEXIBILITY.

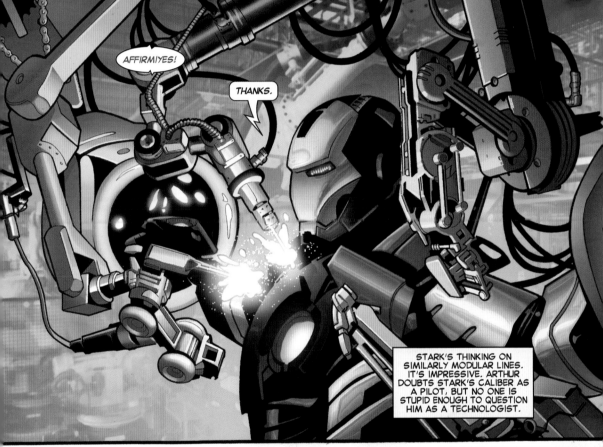

AFFIRMIYES!

THANKS.

STARK'S THINKING ON SIMILARLY MODULAR LINES. IT'S IMPRESSIVE. ARTHUR DOUBTS STARK'S CALIBER AS A PILOT, BUT NO ONE IS STUPID ENOUGH TO QUESTION HIM AS A TECHNOLOGIST.

READY WHEN YOU ARE, WAYNE.

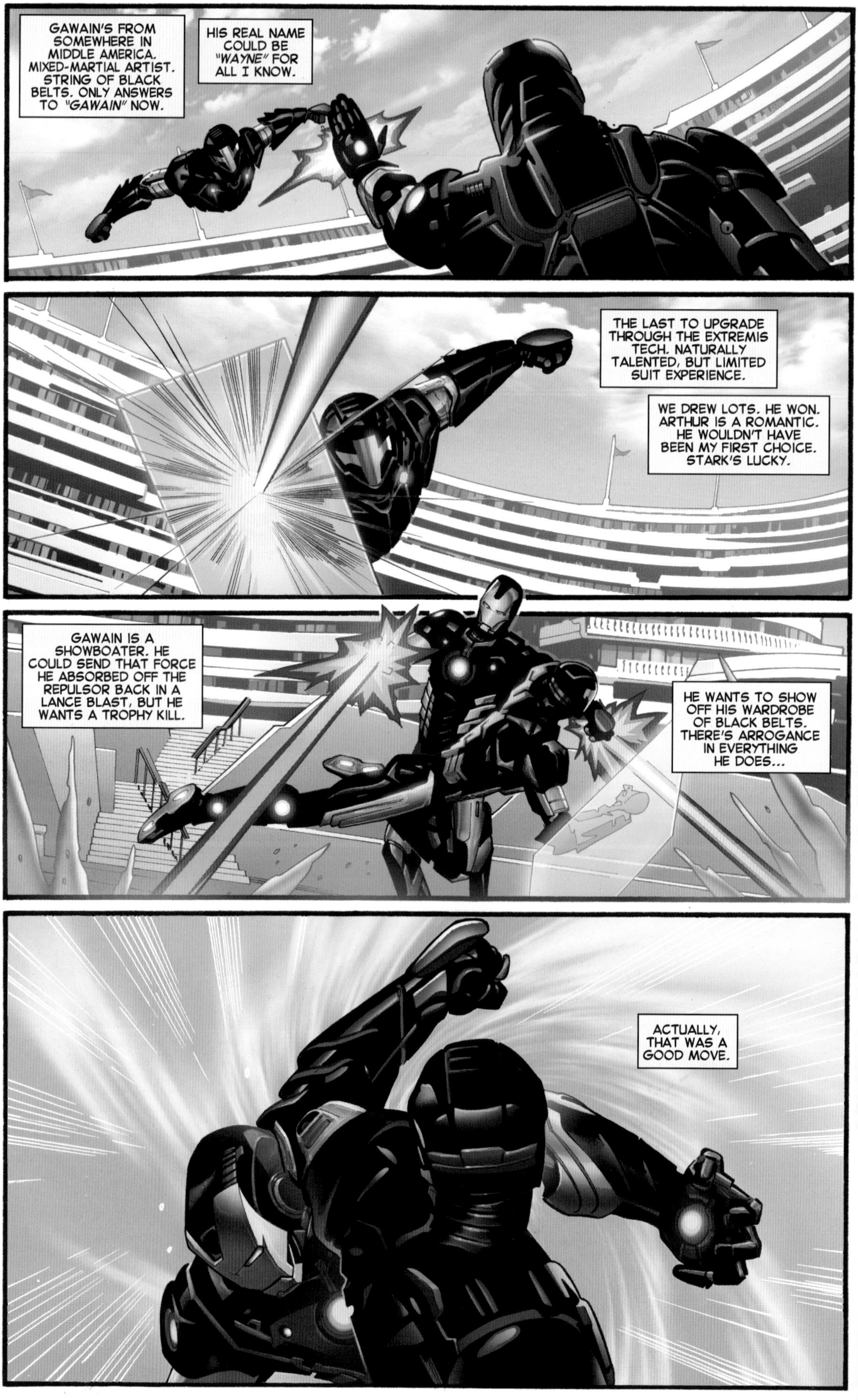
GAWAIN'S FROM SOMEWHERE IN MIDDLE AMERICA. MIXED-MARTIAL ARTIST. STRING OF BLACK BELTS. ONLY ANSWERS TO "GAWAIN" NOW.
HIS REAL NAME COULD BE "WAYNE" FOR ALL I KNOW.
THE LAST TO UPGRADE THROUGH THE EXTREMIS TECH. NATURALLY TALENTED, BUT LIMITED SUIT EXPERIENCE.
WE DREW LOTS. HE WON. ARTHUR IS A ROMANTIC. HE WOULDN'T HAVE BEEN MY FIRST CHOICE. STARK'S LUCKY.
GAWAIN IS A SHOWBOATER. HE COULD SEND THAT FORCE HE ABSORBED OFF THE REPULSOR BACK IN A LANCE BLAST, BUT HE WANTS A TROPHY KILL.
HE WANTS TO SHOW OFF HIS WARDROBE OF BLACK BELTS. THERE'S ARROGANCE IN EVERYTHING HE DOES...
ACTUALLY, THAT WAS A GOOD MOVE.

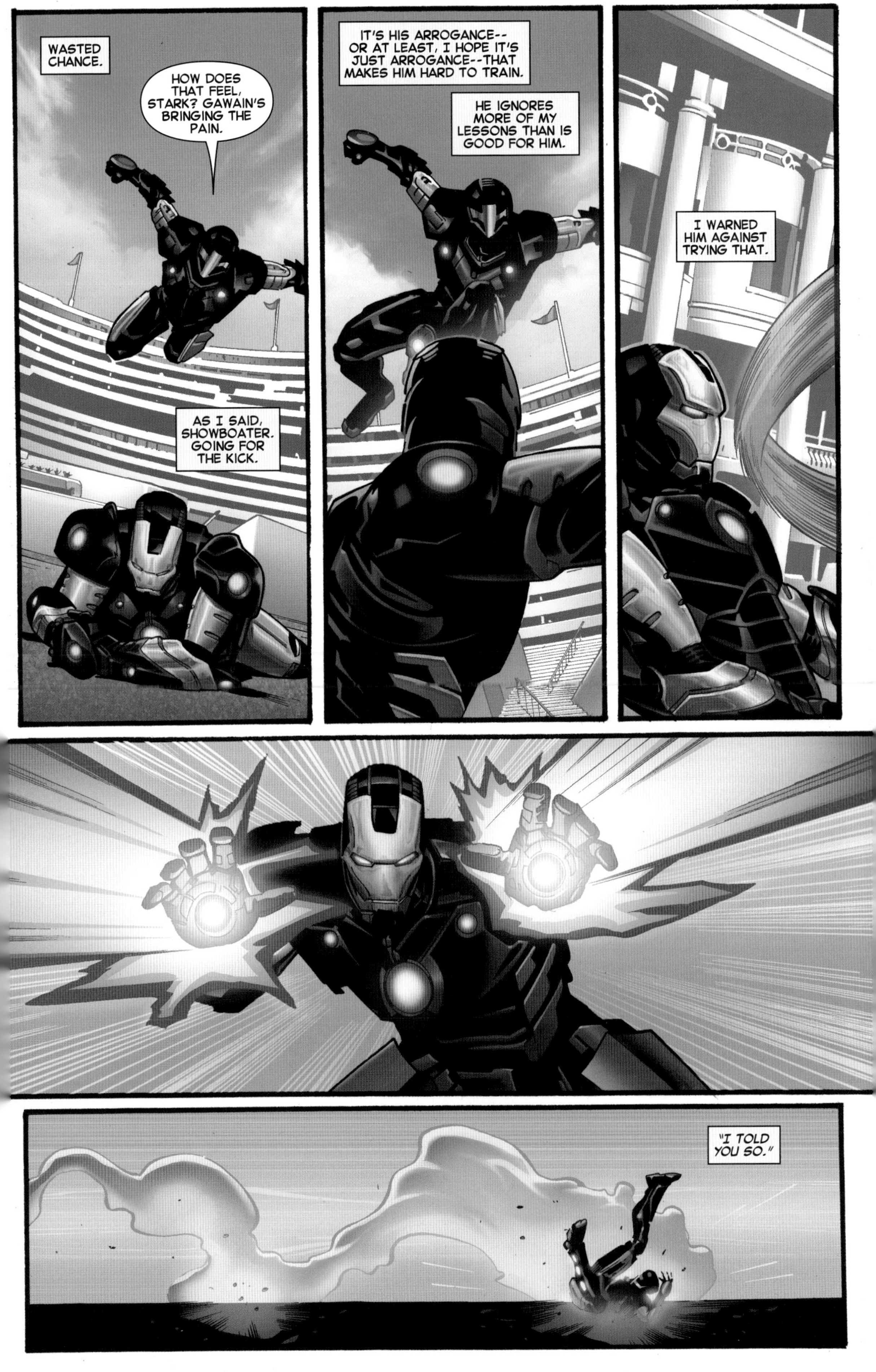
WASTED CHANCE.
HOW DOES THAT FEEL, STARK? GAWAIN'S BRINGING THE PAIN.
AS I SAID, SHOWBOATER. GOING FOR THE KICK.
IT'S HIS ARROGANCE-- OR AT LEAST, I HOPE IT'S JUST ARROGANCE--THAT MAKES HIM HARD TO TRAIN.
HE IGNORES MORE OF MY LESSONS THAN IS GOOD FOR HIM.
I WARNED HIM AGAINST TRYING THAT.
"I TOLD YOU SO."

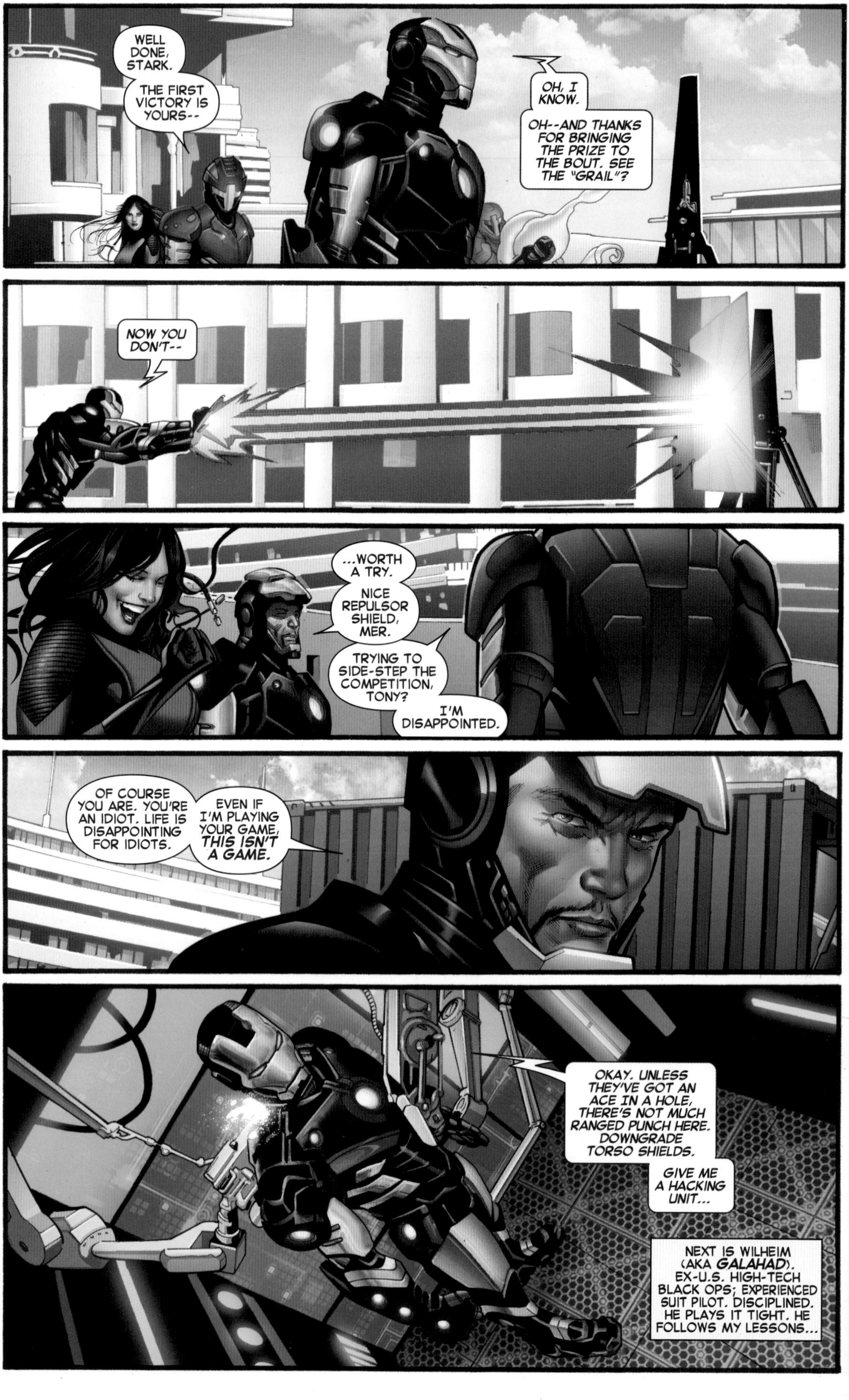
WELL DONE, STARK.
THE FIRST VICTORY IS YOURS--
OH, I KNOW.
OH--AND THANKS FOR BRINGING THE PRIZE TO THE BOUT. SEE THE "GRAIL"?
NOW YOU DON'T--
...WORTH A TRY.
NICE REPULSOR SHIELD, MER.
TRYING TO SIDE-STEP THE COMPETITION, TONY?
I'M DISAPPOINTED.
OF COURSE YOU ARE. YOU'RE AN IDIOT. LIFE IS DISAPPOINTING FOR IDIOTS.
EVEN IF I'M PLAYING YOUR GAME, THIS ISN'T A GAME.
OKAY. UNLESS THEY'VE GOT AN ACE IN A HOLE, THERE'S NOT MUCH RANGED PUNCH HERE. DOWNGRADE TORSO SHIELDS.
GIVE ME A HACKING UNIT...
NEXT IS WILHEIM (AKA GALAHAD). EX-U.S. HIGH-TECH BLACK OPS; EXPERIENCED SUIT PILOT. DISCIPLINED. HE PLAYS IT TIGHT. HE FOLLOWS MY LESSONS...

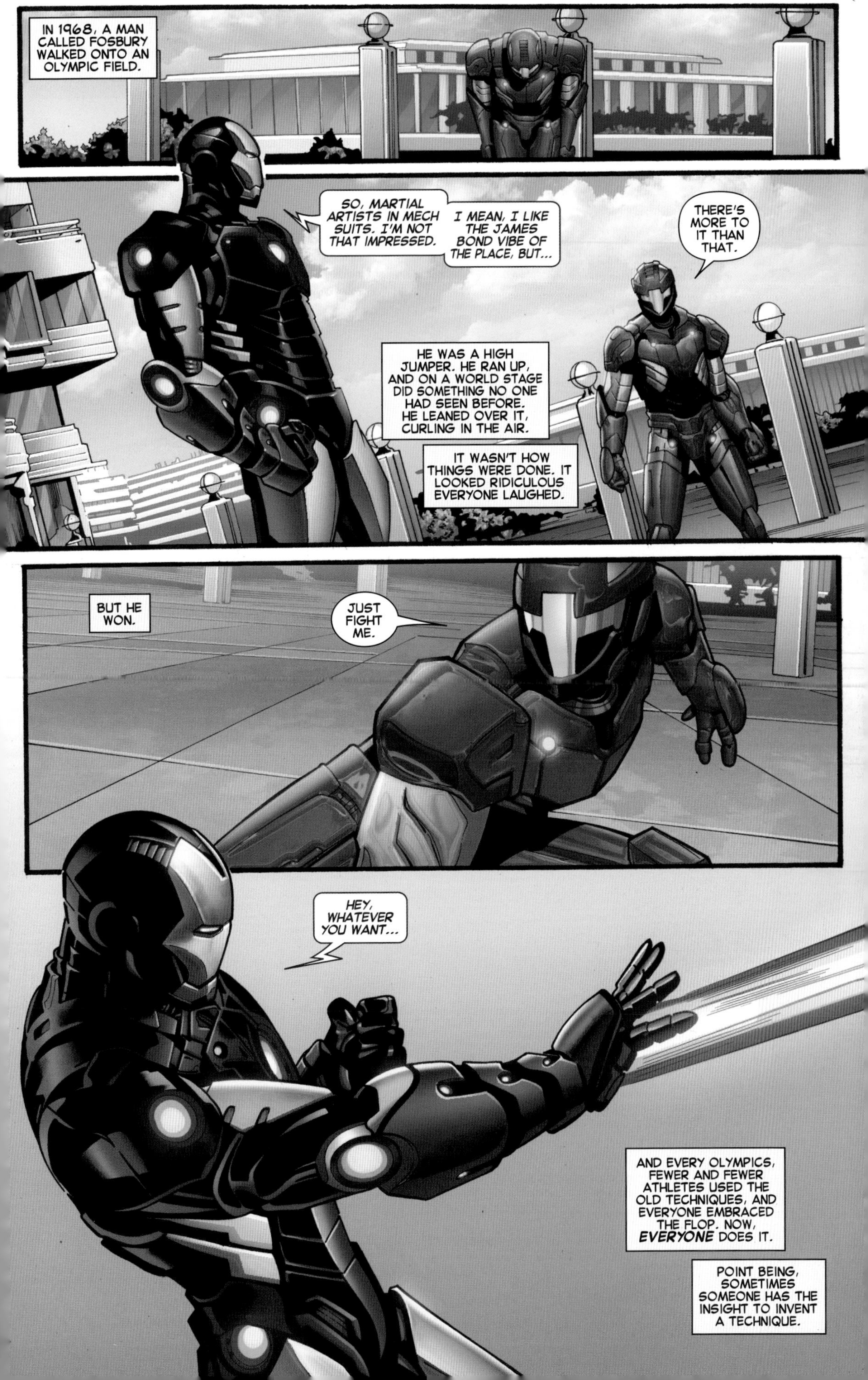
IN 1968, A MAN CALLED FOSBURY WALKED ONTO AN OLYMPIC FIELD.
SO, MARTIAL ARTISTS IN MECH SUITS. I'M NOT THAT IMPRESSED.
I MEAN, I LIKE THE JAMES BOND VIBE OF THE PLACE, BUT...
THERE'S MORE TO IT THAN THAT.
HE WAS A HIGH JUMPER. HE RAN UP, AND ON A WORLD STAGE DID SOMETHING NO ONE HAD SEEN BEFORE. HE LEANED OVER IT, CURLING IN THE AIR.
IT WASN'T HOW THINGS WERE DONE. IT LOOKED RIDICULOUS EVERYONE LAUGHED.
BUT HE WON.
JUST FIGHT ME.
HEY, WHATEVER YOU WANT...
AND EVERY OLYMPICS, FEWER AND FEWER ATHLETES USED THE OLD TECHNIQUES, AND EVERYONE EMBRACED THE FLOP. NOW, EVERYONE DOES IT.
POINT BEING, SOMETIMES SOMEONE HAS THE INSIGHT TO INVENT A TECHNIQUE.

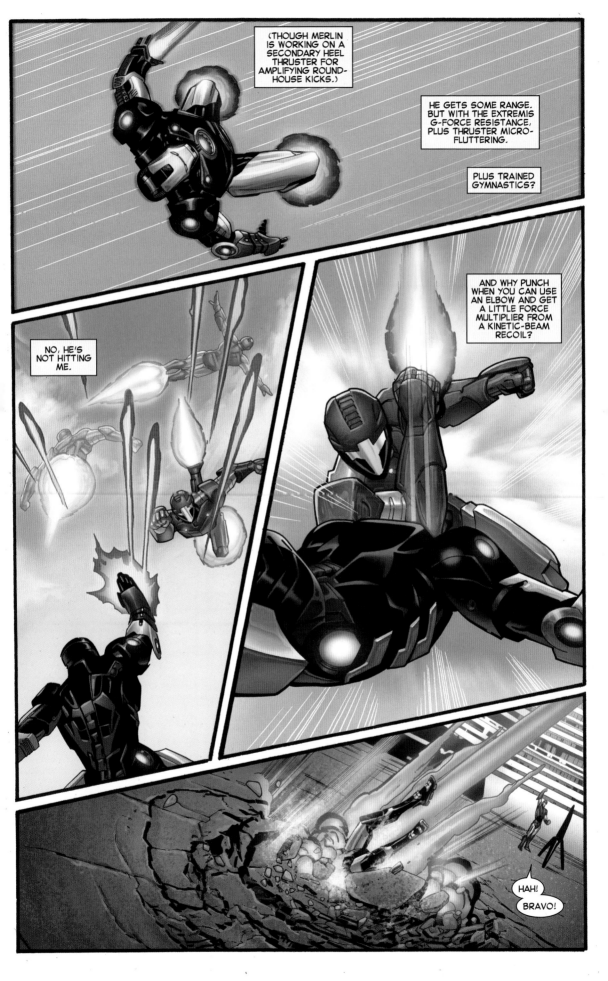

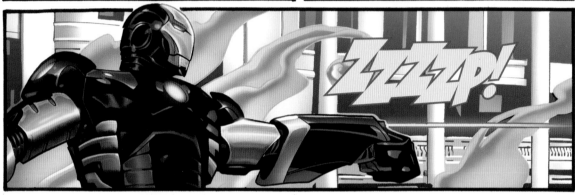

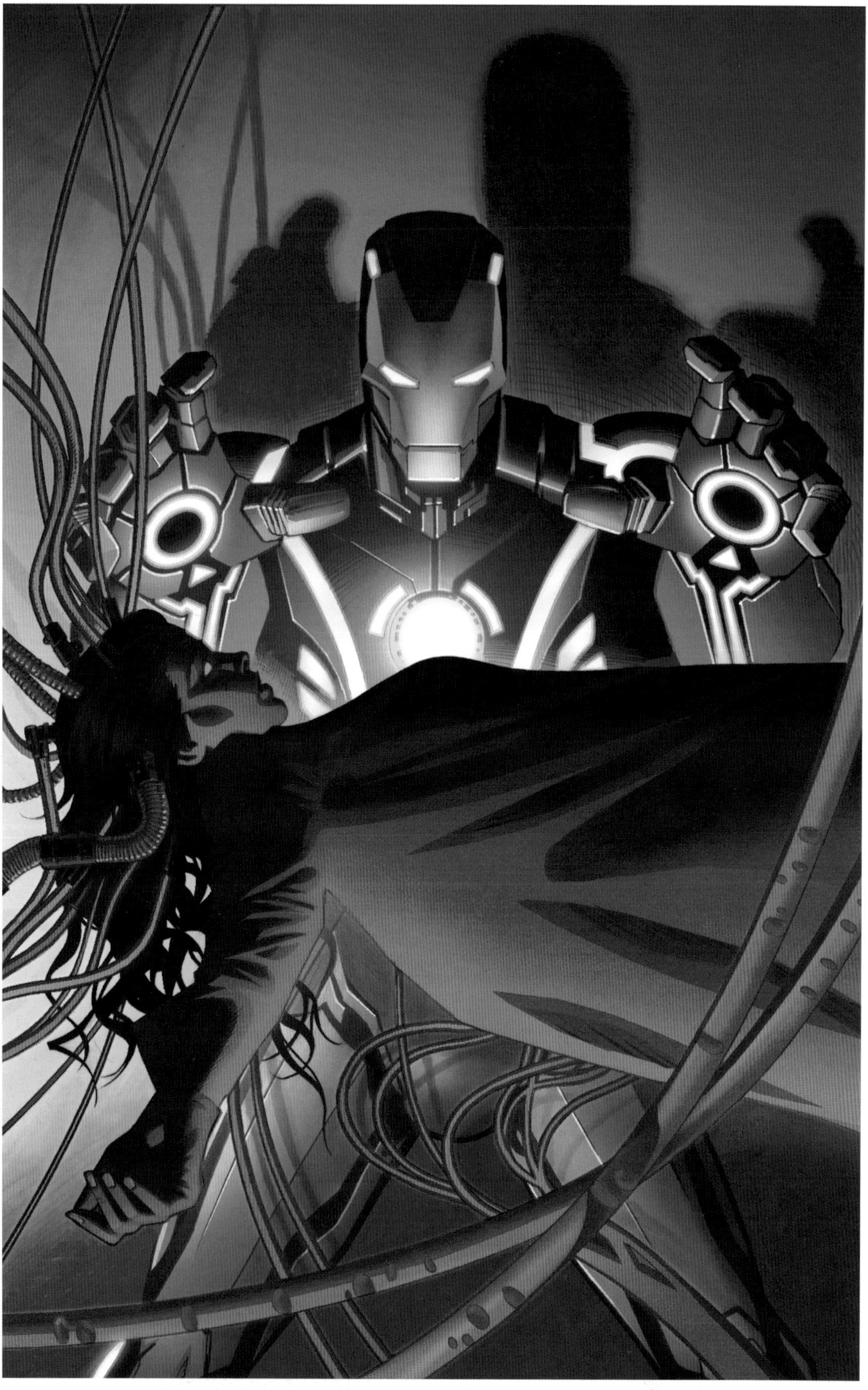

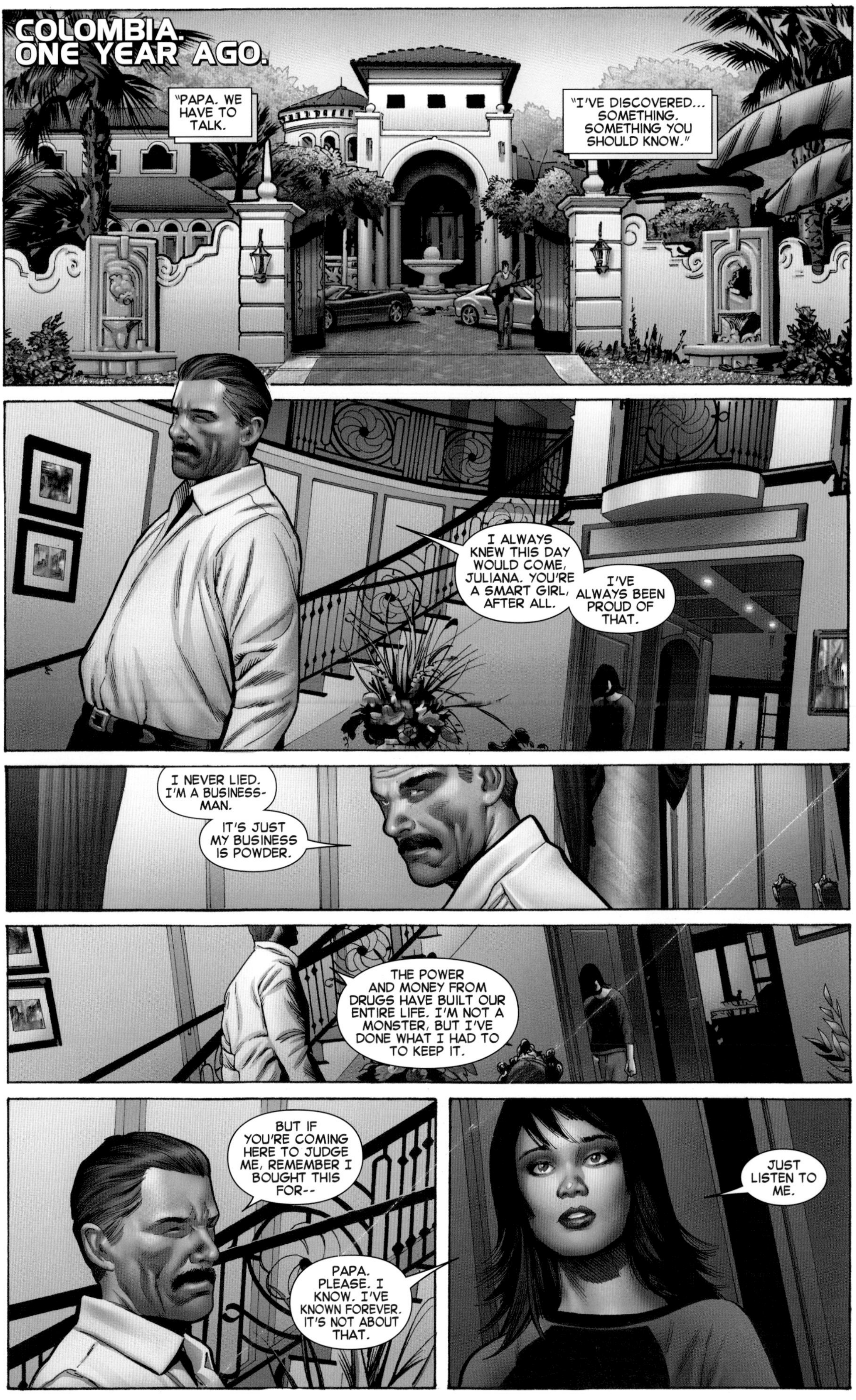
COLOMBIA. ONE YEAR AGO.
"PAPA. WE HAVE TO TALK.
"I'VE DISCOVERED... SOMETHING. SOMETHING YOU SHOULD KNOW."
I ALWAYS KNEW THIS DAY WOULD COME, JULIANA. YOU'RE A SMART GIRL, AFTER ALL.
I'VE ALWAYS BEEN PROUD OF THAT.
I NEVER LIED. I'M A BUSINESS-MAN.
IT'S JUST MY BUSINESS IS POWDER.
THE POWER AND MONEY FROM DRUGS HAVE BUILT OUR ENTIRE LIFE. I'M NOT A MONSTER, BUT I'VE DONE WHAT I HAD TO TO KEEP IT.
BUT IF YOU'RE COMING HERE TO JUDGE ME, REMEMBER I BOUGHT THIS FOR--
PAPA. PLEASE. I KNOW. I'VE KNOWN FOREVER. IT'S NOT ABOUT THAT.
JUST LISTEN TO ME.

TONY. I *REALLY* DON'T UNDERSTAND WHAT YOU'RE DOING NOW...

ISN'T IT OBVIOUS, FUTURE CEO-OF-THE-YEAR PEPPER POTTS? I'M PREPARING GRILLED CHEESE ON TOAST... IN A MICROWAVE.

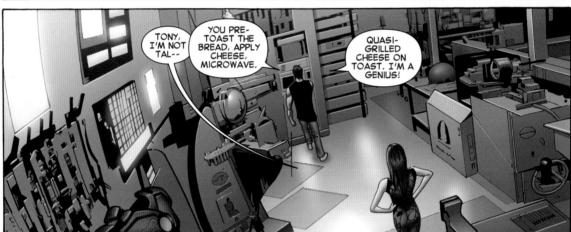

TONY, I'M NOT TAL--

YOU PRE-TOAST THE BREAD, APPLY CHEESE, MICROWAVE.

QUASI-GRILLED CHEESE ON TOAST. I'M A GENIUS!

TONY! BE SERIOUS! I'M TALKING ABOUT--

I'M A MAN OF SCIENCE, PEPPER. DON'T STAND IN THE WAY OF SCIENCE.

IT MAY NOT BE RIGHT. IT MAY DEFY ALL NATURAL LAW, BUT I'M GOING TO DO IT ANYWAY.

AFTER WHAT I DID FOR THE MILITARY, CAN YOU HONESTLY SAY THIS IS ANY WORSE? DO NOT JUDGE ME, POTTS.

I MEANT WHAT ARE YOU DOING WITH ALL THE NEW MODULAR SUITS?

YOUR LAST ARMOR WAS BASED ON *LIQUID* TECH AND *SMART* METALS. ISN'T THIS A STEP BACK?

OH, *THAT*.

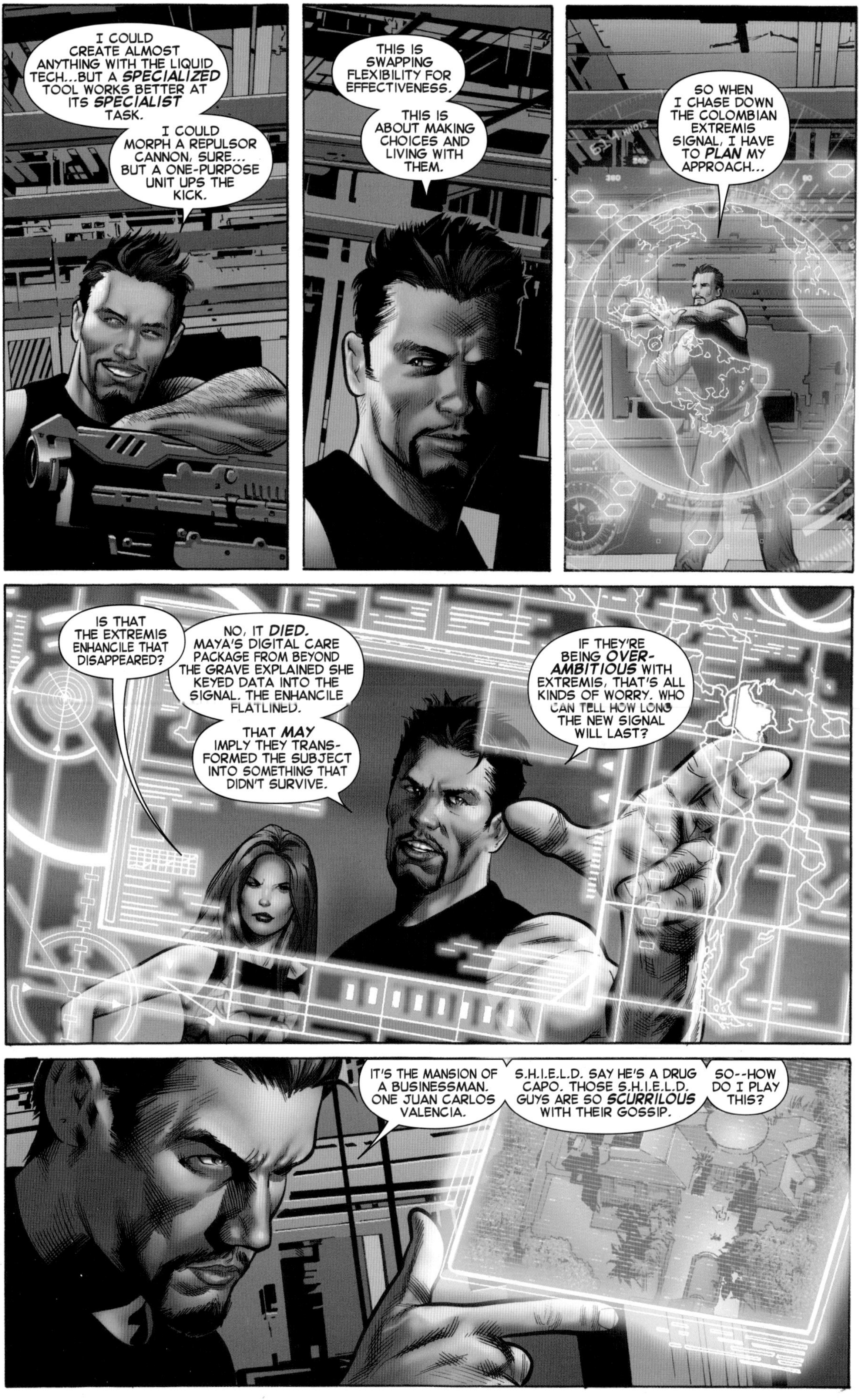

I COULD CREATE ALMOST ANYTHING WITH THE LIQUID TECH...BUT A SPECIALIZED TOOL WORKS BETTER AT ITS SPECIALIST TASK.
I COULD MORPH A REPULSOR CANNON, SURE... BUT A ONE-PURPOSE UNIT UPS THE KICK.
THIS IS SWAPPING FLEXIBILITY FOR EFFECTIVENESS.
THIS IS ABOUT MAKING CHOICES AND LIVING WITH THEM.
SO WHEN I CHASE DOWN THE COLOMBIAN EXTREMIS SIGNAL, I HAVE TO PLAN MY APPROACH...
IS THAT THE EXTREMIS ENHANCILE THAT DISAPPEARED?
NO, IT DIED. MAYA'S DIGITAL CARE PACKAGE FROM BEYOND THE GRAVE EXPLAINED SHE KEYED DATA INTO THE SIGNAL. THE ENHANCILE FLATLINED.
THAT MAY IMPLY THEY TRANS-FORMED THE SUBJECT INTO SOMETHING THAT DIDN'T SURVIVE.
IF THEY'RE BEING OVER-AMBITIOUS WITH EXTREMIS, THAT'S ALL KINDS OF WORRY. WHO CAN TELL HOW LONG THE NEW SIGNAL WILL LAST?
IT'S THE MANSION OF A BUSINESSMAN. ONE JUAN CARLOS VALENCIA.
S.H.I.E.L.D. SAY HE'S A DRUG CAPO. THOSE S.H.I.E.L.D. GUYS ARE SO SCURRILOUS WITH THEIR GOSSIP.
SO--HOW DO I PLAY THIS?

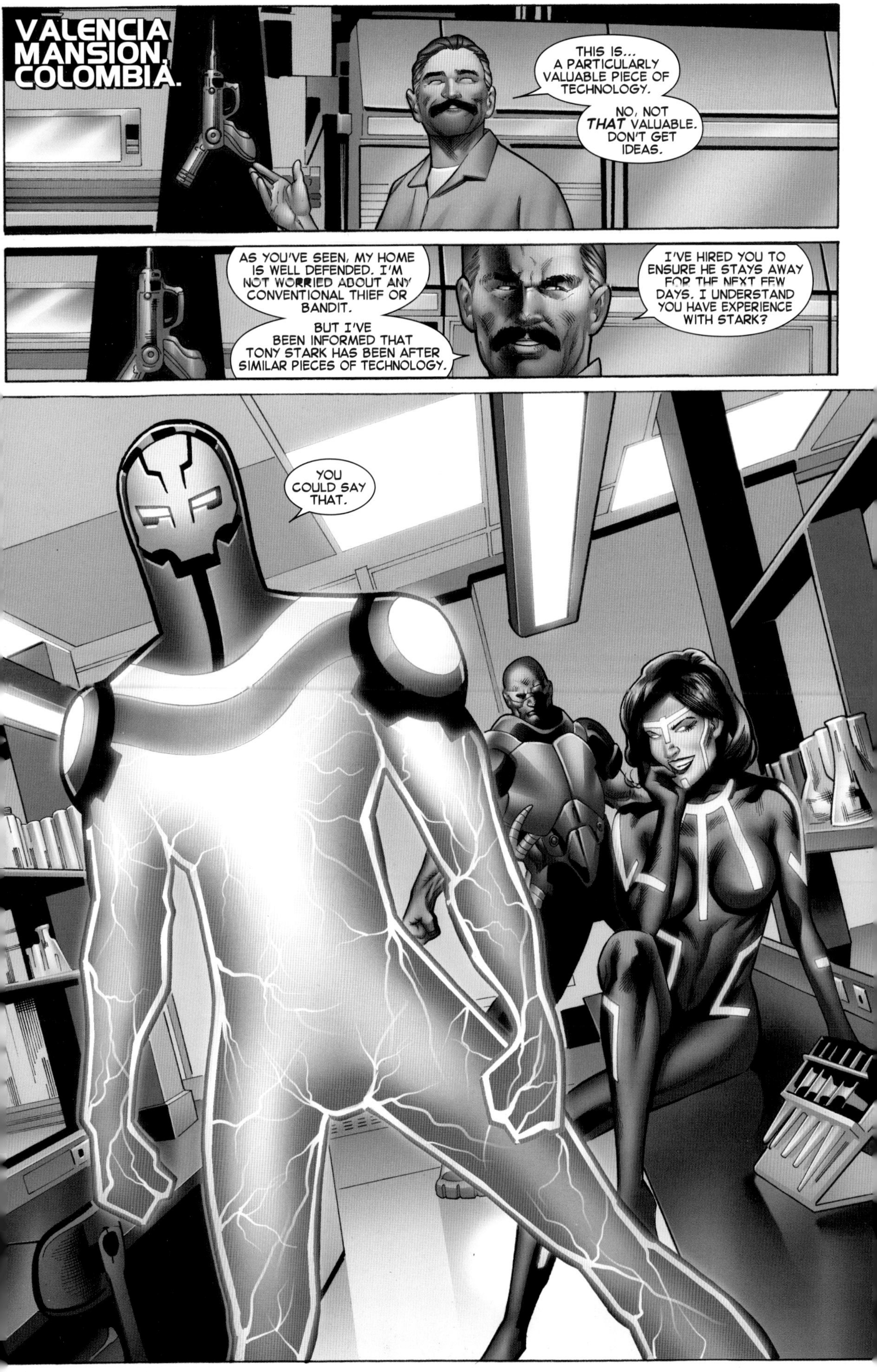
VALENCIA MANSION, COLOMBIA.
THIS IS... A PARTICULARLY VALUABLE PIECE OF TECHNOLOGY.
NO, NOT THAT VALUABLE. DON'T GET IDEAS.
AS YOU'VE SEEN, MY HOME IS WELL DEFENDED. I'M NOT WORRIED ABOUT ANY CONVENTIONAL THIEF OR BANDIT.
BUT I'VE BEEN INFORMED THAT TONY STARK HAS BEEN AFTER SIMILAR PIECES OF TECHNOLOGY.
I'VE HIRED YOU TO ENSURE HE STAYS AWAY FOR THE NEXT FEW DAYS. I UNDERSTAND YOU HAVE EXPERIENCE WITH STARK?
YOU COULD SAY THAT.

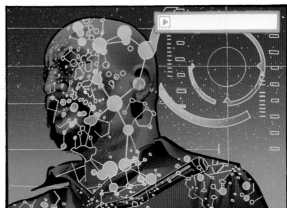

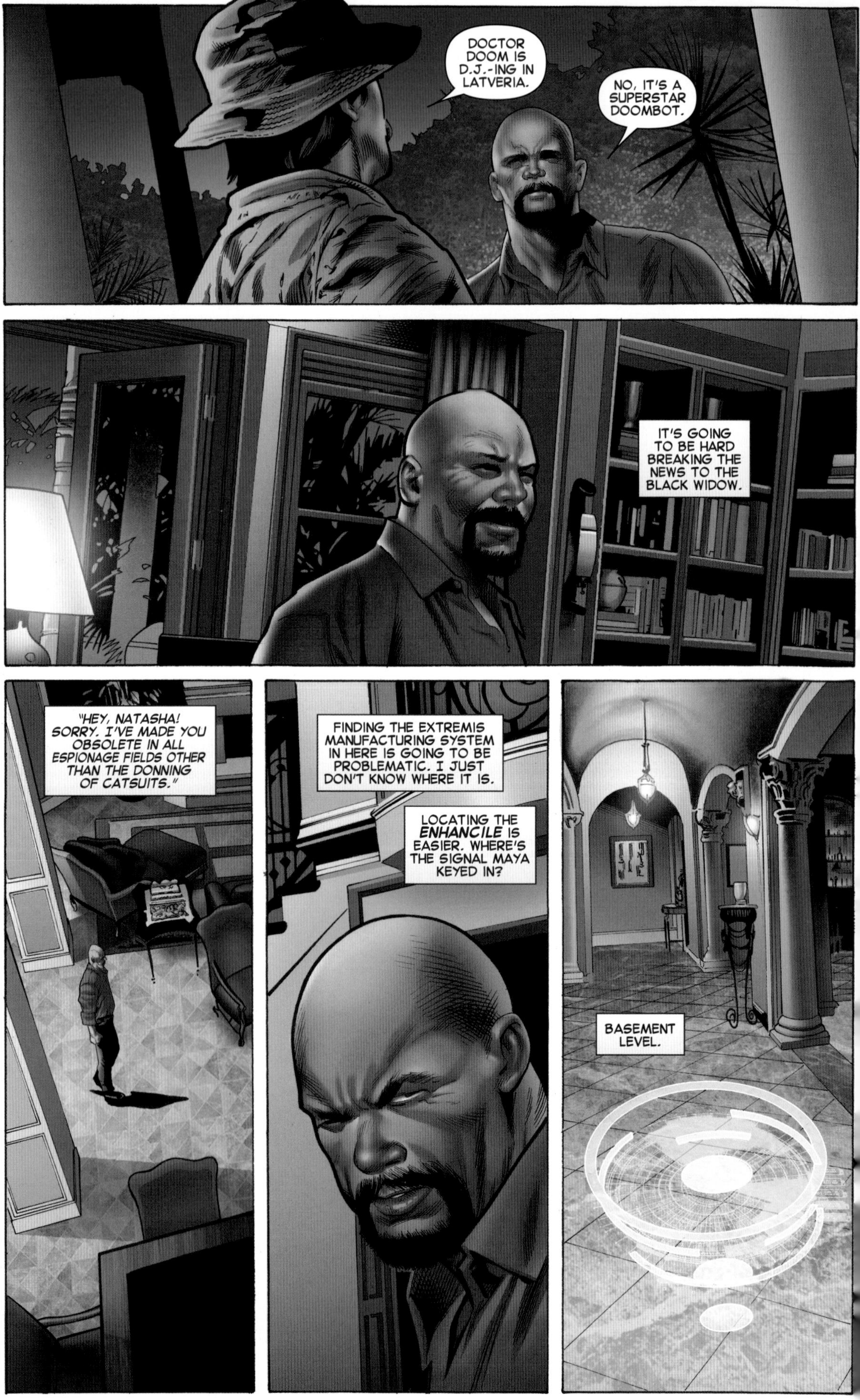
DOCTOR DOOM IS D.J.-ING IN LATVERIA.
NO, IT'S A SUPERSTAR DOOMBOT.
IT'S GOING TO BE HARD BREAKING THE NEWS TO THE BLACK WIDOW.
"HEY, NATASHA! SORRY. I'VE MADE YOU OBSOLETE IN ALL ESPIONAGE FIELDS OTHER THAN THE DONNING OF CATSUITS."
FINDING THE EXTREMIS MANUFACTURING SYSTEM IN HERE IS GOING TO BE PROBLEMATIC. I JUST DON'T KNOW WHERE IT IS.
LOCATING THE ENHANCILE IS EASIER. WHERE'S THE SIGNAL MAYA KEYED IN?
BASEMENT LEVEL.

CROSS-REFERENCE SIGNAL WITH ORBITAL SATELLITE SCANS...

GIVE ME THE BEST ROUTE.

AFFIRMATIVE.

THANK YOU.

LABORATORIES? HMM.

THE ENHANCILE'S INSIDE. EXPENSIVE LOCK. VERY NICE.

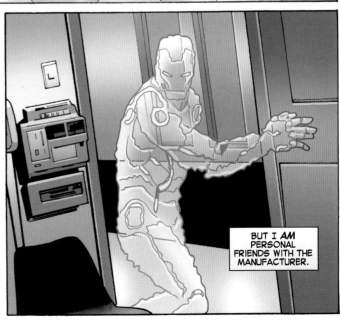

BUT I AM PERSONAL FRIENDS WITH THE MANUFACTURER.

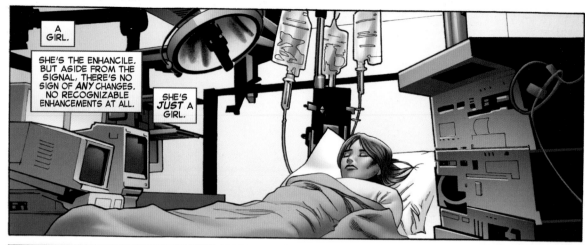

A GIRL.

SHE'S THE ENHANCILE. BUT ASIDE FROM THE SIGNAL, THERE'S NO SIGN OF *ANY* CHANGES. NO RECOGNIZABLE ENHANCEMENTS AT ALL.

SHE'S *JUST* A GIRL.

SHE'S A VICTIM. SHE HAS TO BE. THEY'RE RUNNING SOME KIND OF EXPERIMENT.

TIME TO TAKE A CHANCE...

I'M IRON MAN. I'M HERE TO SAVE YOU. DO YOU REMEMBER WHERE THEY PERFORMED THE OPERATION?

GUARDS!

SORRY, NATASHA.

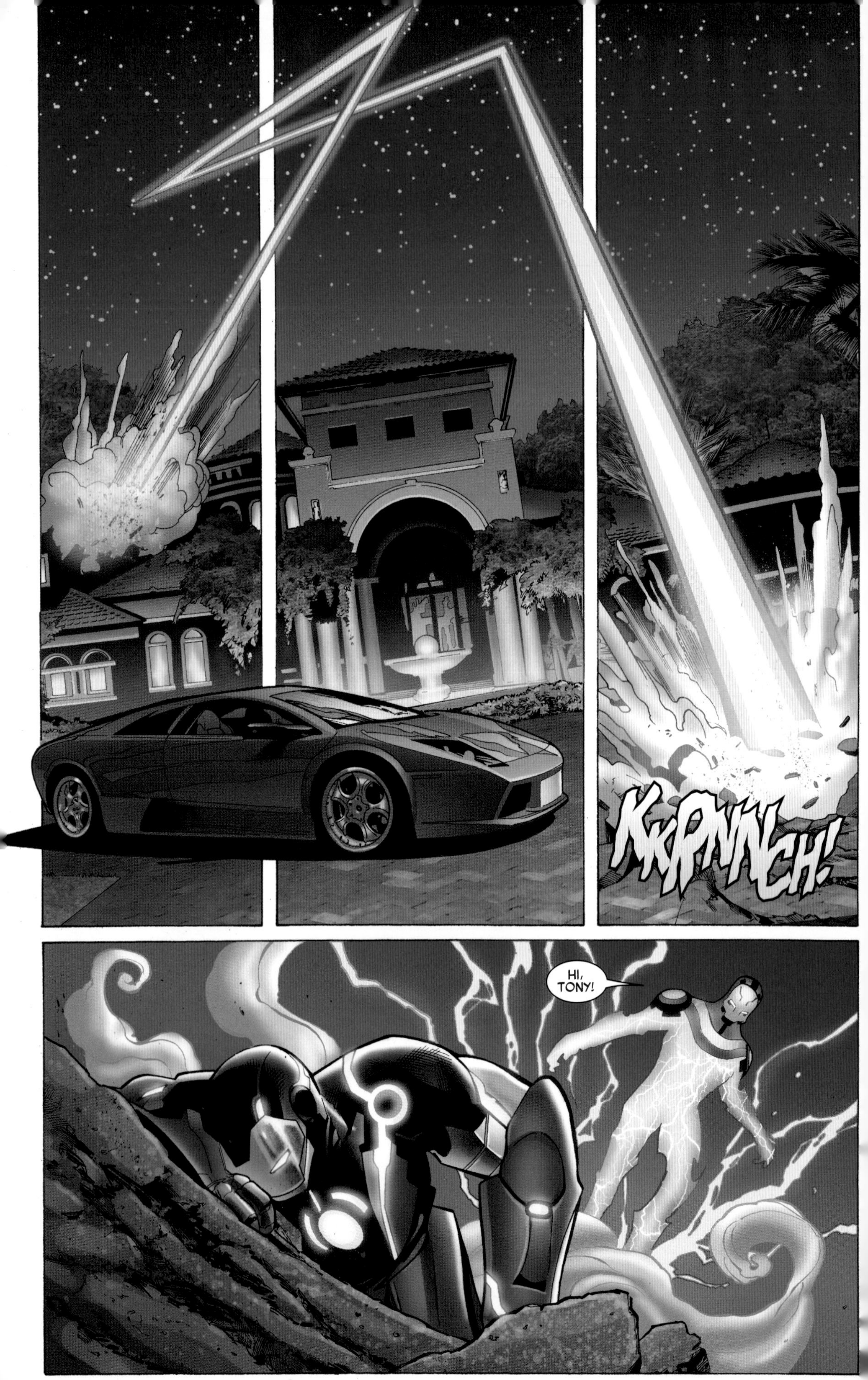
KKRUNNCH!
HI, TONY!

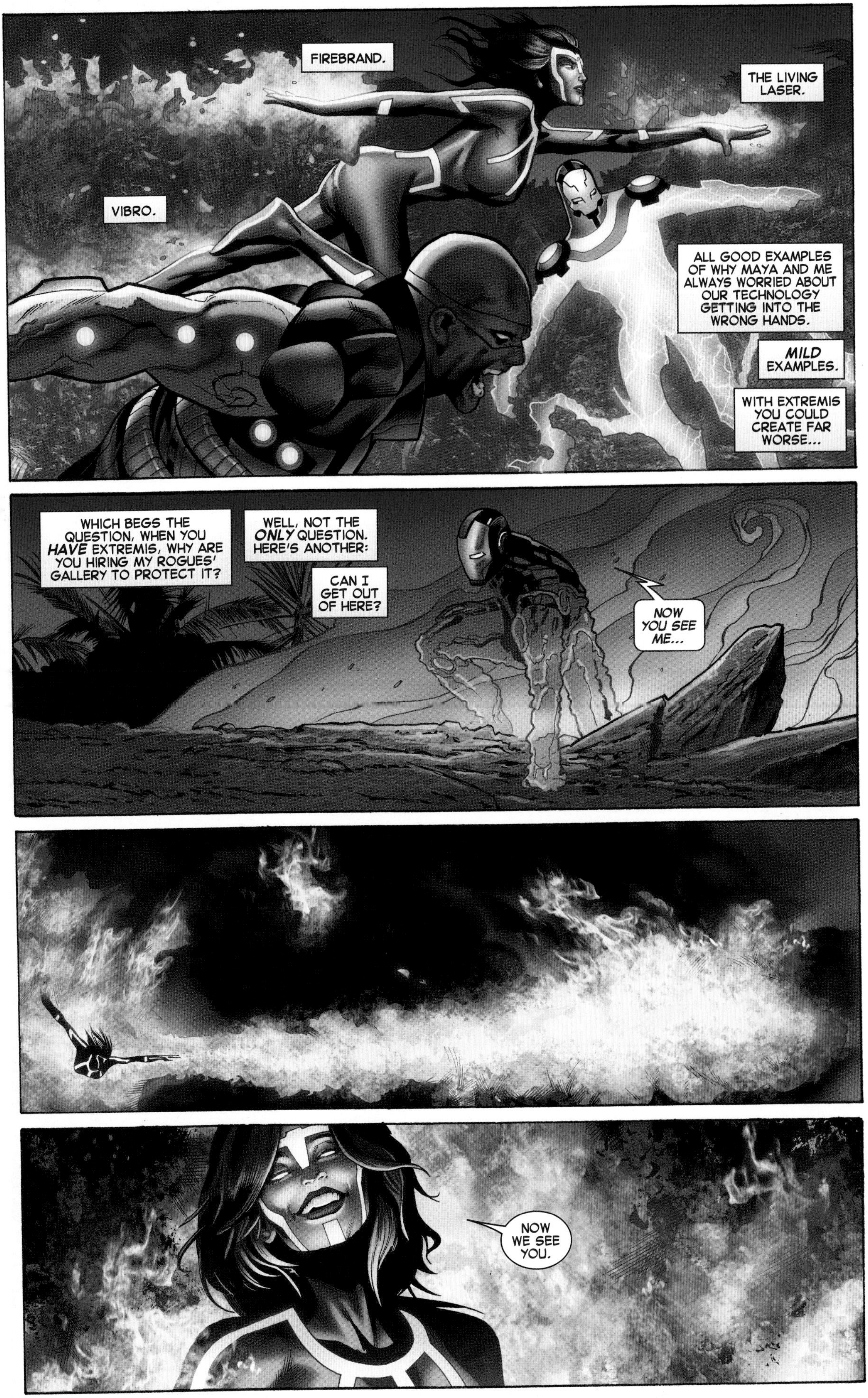
FIREBRAND.
THE LIVING LASER.
VIBRO.
ALL GOOD EXAMPLES OF WHY MAYA AND ME ALWAYS WORRIED ABOUT OUR TECHNOLOGY GETTING INTO THE WRONG HANDS.
MILD EXAMPLES.
WITH EXTREMIS YOU COULD CREATE FAR WORSE...
WHICH BEGS THE QUESTION, WHEN YOU HAVE EXTREMIS, WHY ARE YOU HIRING MY ROGUES' GALLERY TO PROTECT IT?
WELL, NOT THE ONLY QUESTION. HERE'S ANOTHER:
CAN I GET OUT OF HERE?
NOW YOU SEE ME...
NOW WE SEE YOU.

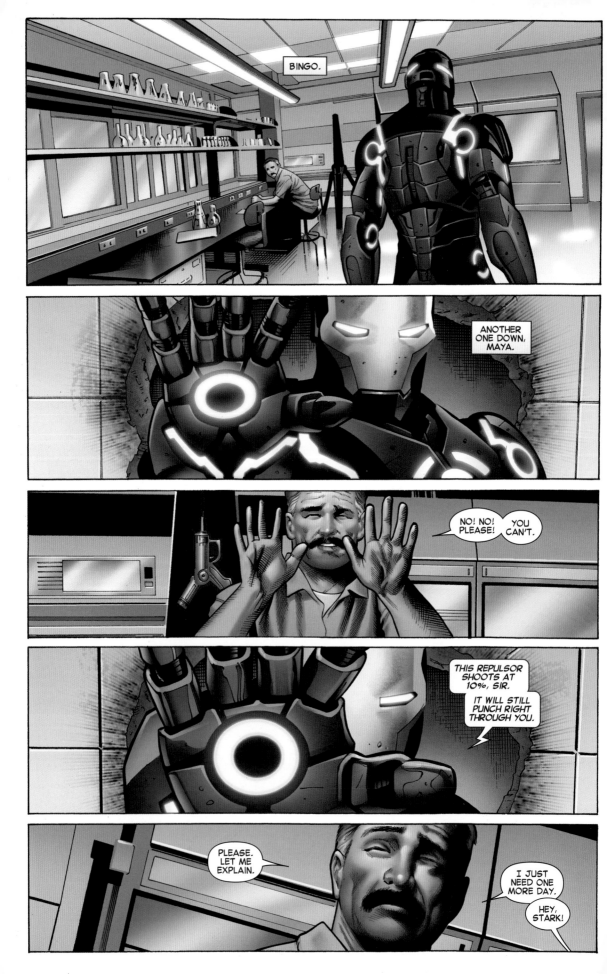

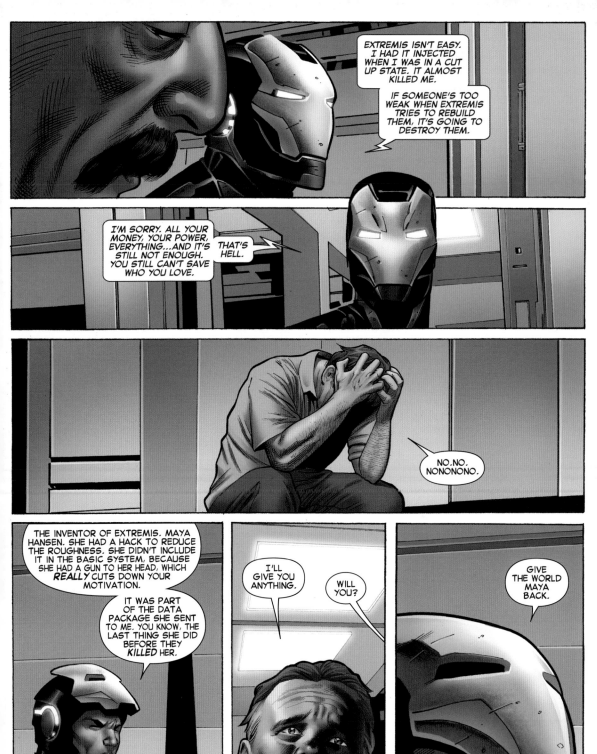

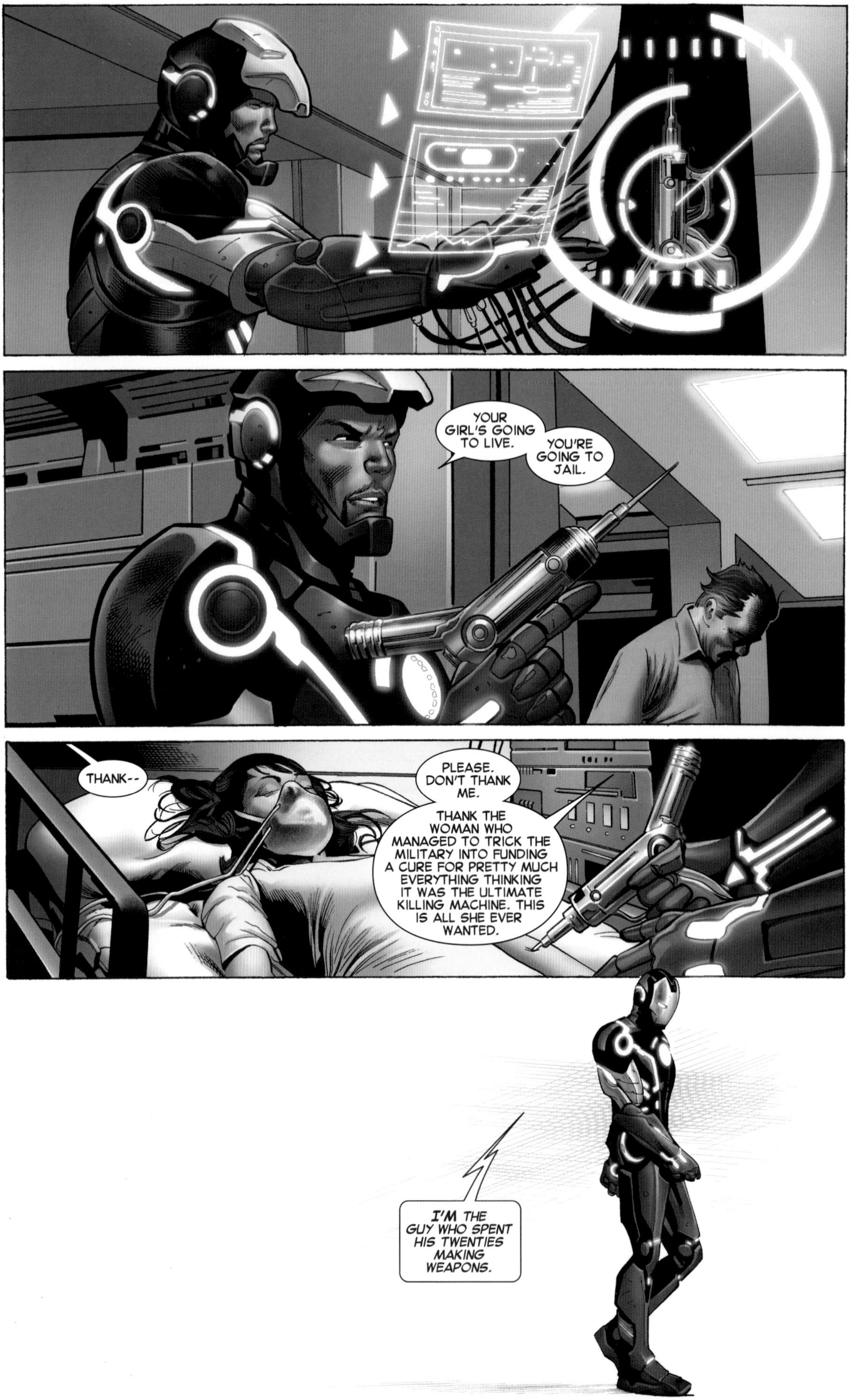
YOUR GIRL'S GOING TO LIVE.
YOU'RE GOING TO JAIL.
THANK--
PLEASE. DON'T THANK ME.
THANK THE WOMAN WHO MANAGED TO TRICK THE MILITARY INTO FUNDING A CURE FOR PRETTY MUCH EVERYTHING THINKING IT WAS THE ULTIMATE KILLING MACHINE. THIS IS ALL SHE EVER WANTED.
I'M THE GUY WHO SPENT HIS TWENTIES MAKING WEAPONS.

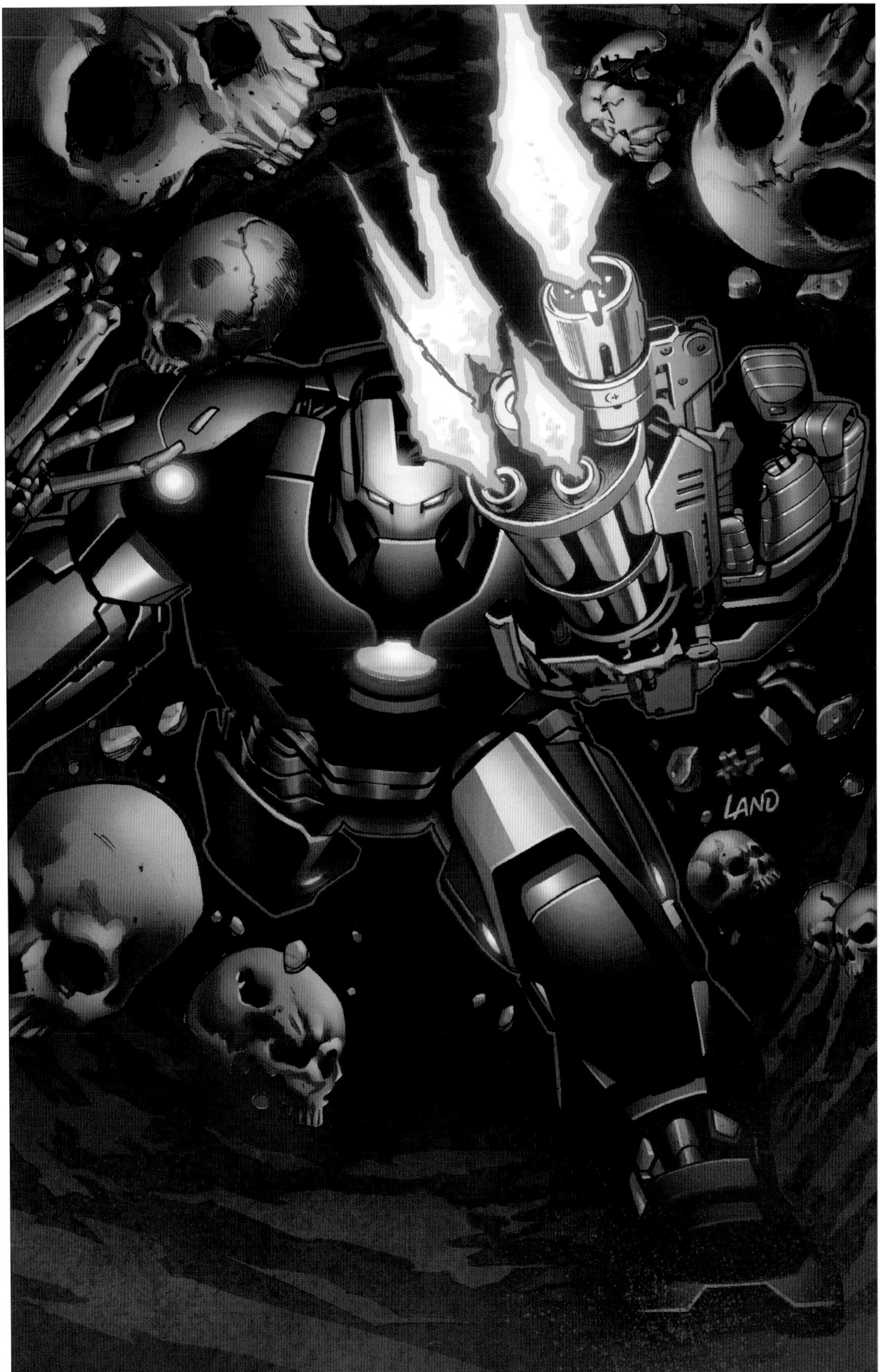
LAND

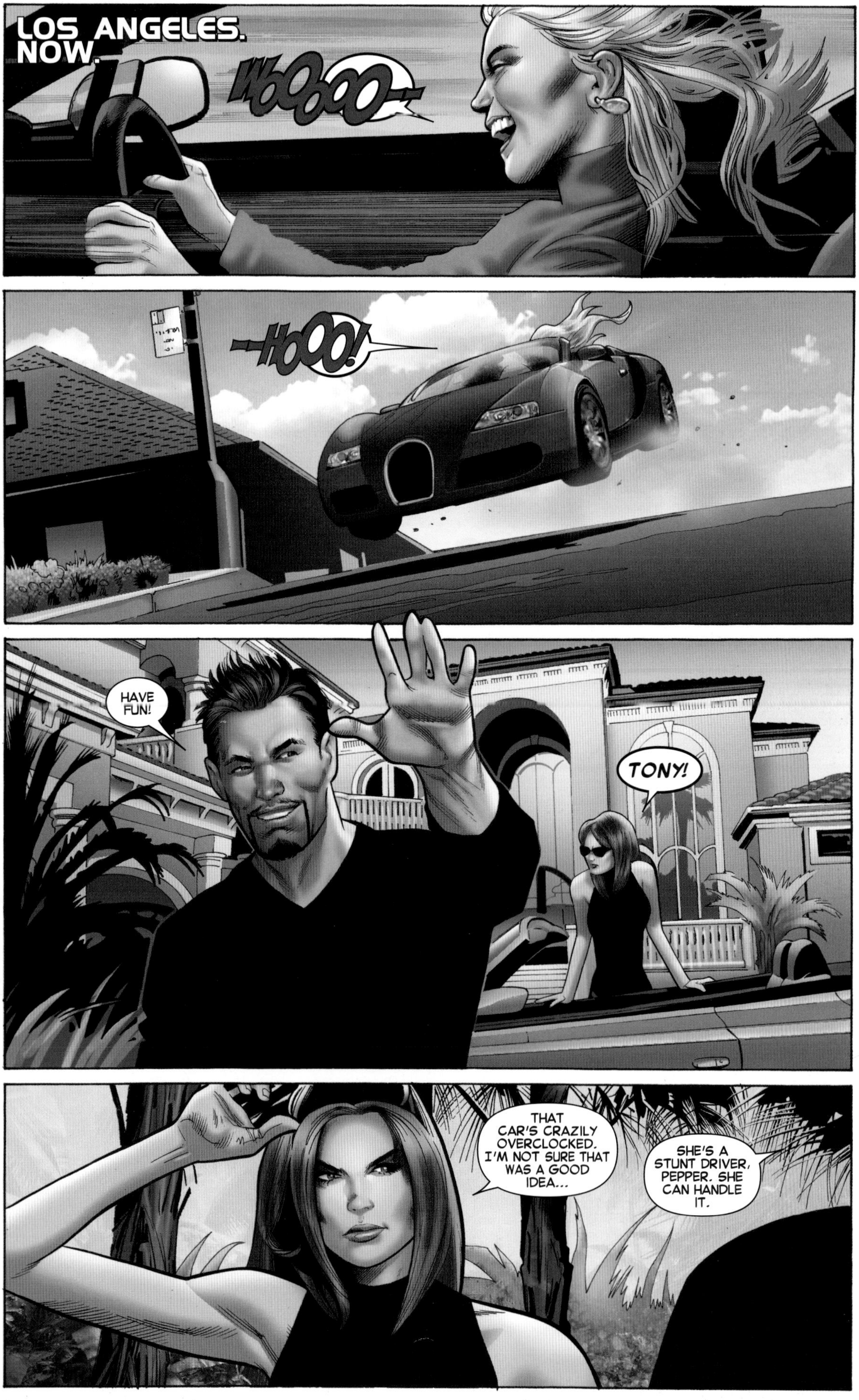
LOS ANGELES. NOW.
WOOOOO--
--HOOO!
HAVE FUN!
TONY!
THAT CAR'S CRAZILY OVERCLOCKED. I'M NOT SURE THAT WAS A GOOD IDEA...
SHE'S A STUNT DRIVER, PEPPER. SHE CAN HANDLE IT.

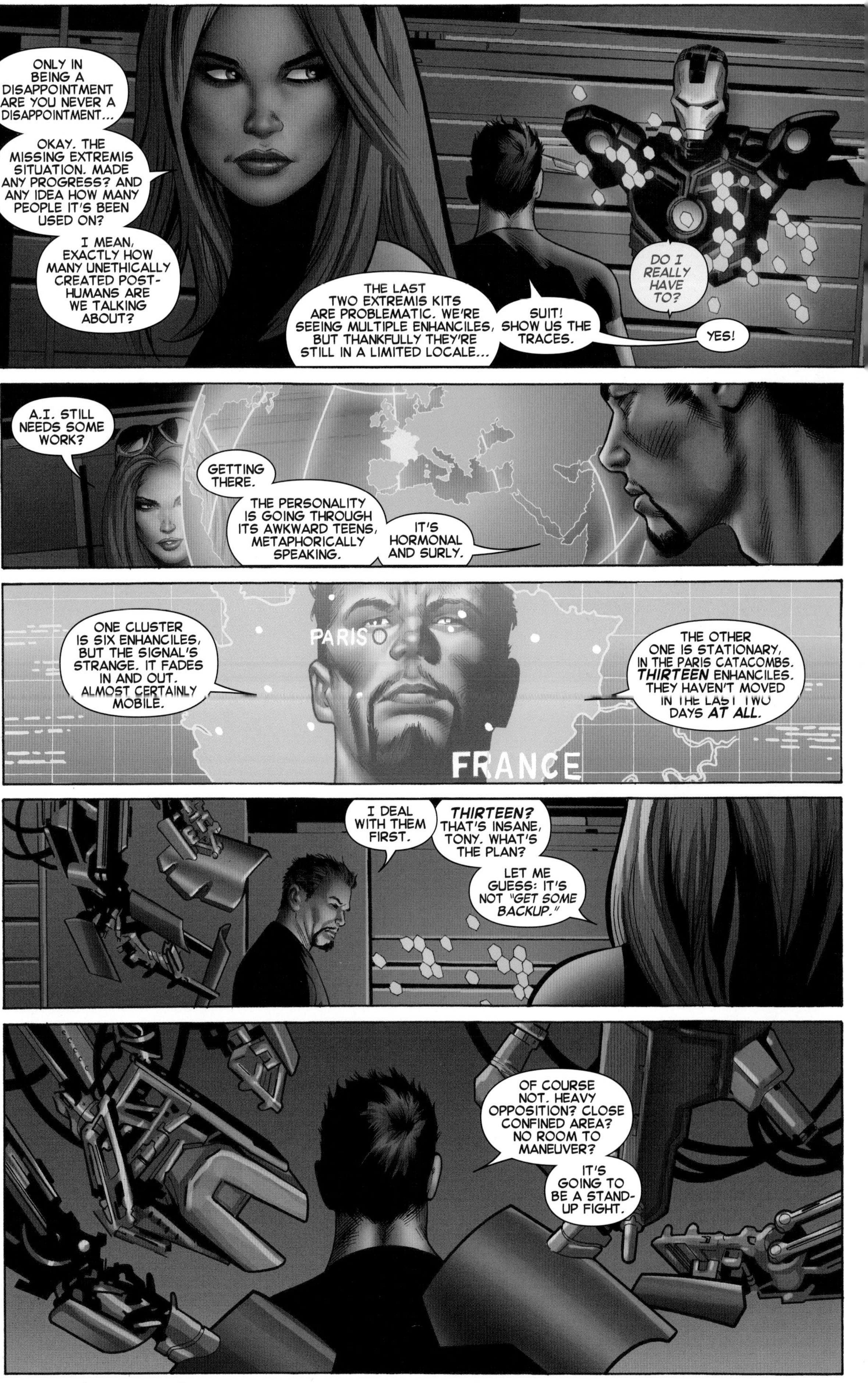
ONLY IN BEING A DISAPPOINTMENT ARE YOU NEVER A DISAPPOINTMENT...
OKAY. THE MISSING EXTREMIS SITUATION. MADE ANY PROGRESS? AND ANY IDEA HOW MANY PEOPLE IT'S BEEN USED ON?
I MEAN, EXACTLY HOW MANY UNETHICALLY CREATED POST-HUMANS ARE WE TALKING ABOUT?
THE LAST TWO EXTREMIS KITS ARE PROBLEMATIC. WE'RE SEEING MULTIPLE ENHANCILES, BUT THANKFULLY THEY'RE STILL IN A LIMITED LOCALE...
SUIT! SHOW US THE TRACES.
DO I REALLY HAVE TO?
YES!
A.I. STILL NEEDS SOME WORK?
GETTING THERE.
THE PERSONALITY IS GOING THROUGH ITS AWKWARD TEENS, METAPHORICALLY SPEAKING.
IT'S HORMONAL AND SURLY.
PARIS
ONE CLUSTER IS SIX ENHANCILES, BUT THE SIGNAL'S STRANGE. IT FADES IN AND OUT. ALMOST CERTAINLY MOBILE.
THE OTHER ONE IS STATIONARY, IN THE PARIS CATACOMBS. THIRTEEN ENHANCILES. THEY HAVEN'T MOVED IN THE LAST TWO DAYS AT ALL.
FRANCE
I DEAL WITH THEM FIRST.
THIRTEEN? THAT'S INSANE, TONY. WHAT'S THE PLAN?
LET ME GUESS: IT'S NOT "GET SOME BACKUP."
OF COURSE NOT. HEAVY OPPOSITION? CLOSE CONFINED AREA? NO ROOM TO MANEUVER?
IT'S GOING TO BE A STAND-UP FIGHT.

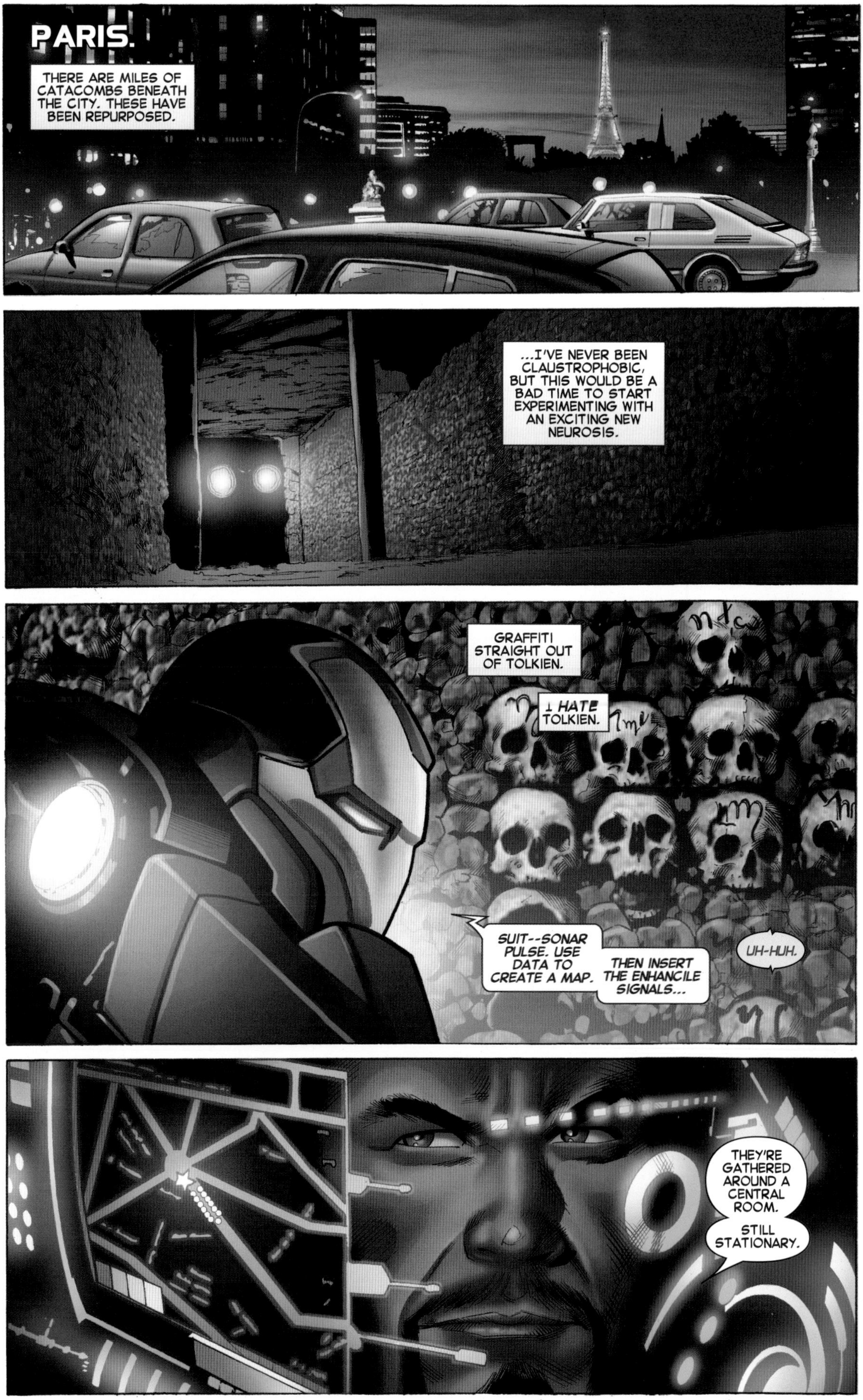
PARIS.
THERE ARE MILES OF CATACOMBS BENEATH THE CITY. THESE HAVE BEEN REPURPOSED.
...I'VE NEVER BEEN CLAUSTROPHOBIC, BUT THIS WOULD BE A BAD TIME TO START EXPERIMENTING WITH AN EXCITING NEW NEUROSIS.
GRAFFITI STRAIGHT OUT OF TOLKIEN.
I HATE TOLKIEN.
SUIT--SONAR PULSE. USE DATA TO CREATE A MAP.
THEN INSERT THE ENHANCILE SIGNALS...
UH-HUH.
THEY'RE GATHERED AROUND A CENTRAL ROOM.
STILL STATIONARY.

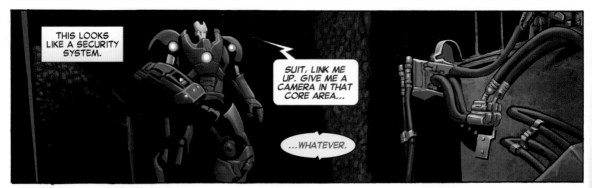

THIS LOOKS LIKE A SECURITY SYSTEM.

SUIT, LINK ME UP. GIVE ME A CAMERA IN THAT CORE AREA...

...WHATEVER.

THERE WE GO. SIXTY METERS...

THE MISSING EXTREMIS SYSTEM.

AND A... SCIENTIST? ARMED. AND SCARED.

ANY OTHER CAMERAS?

YEAH.

GIVE THEM TO ME.

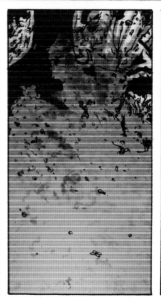

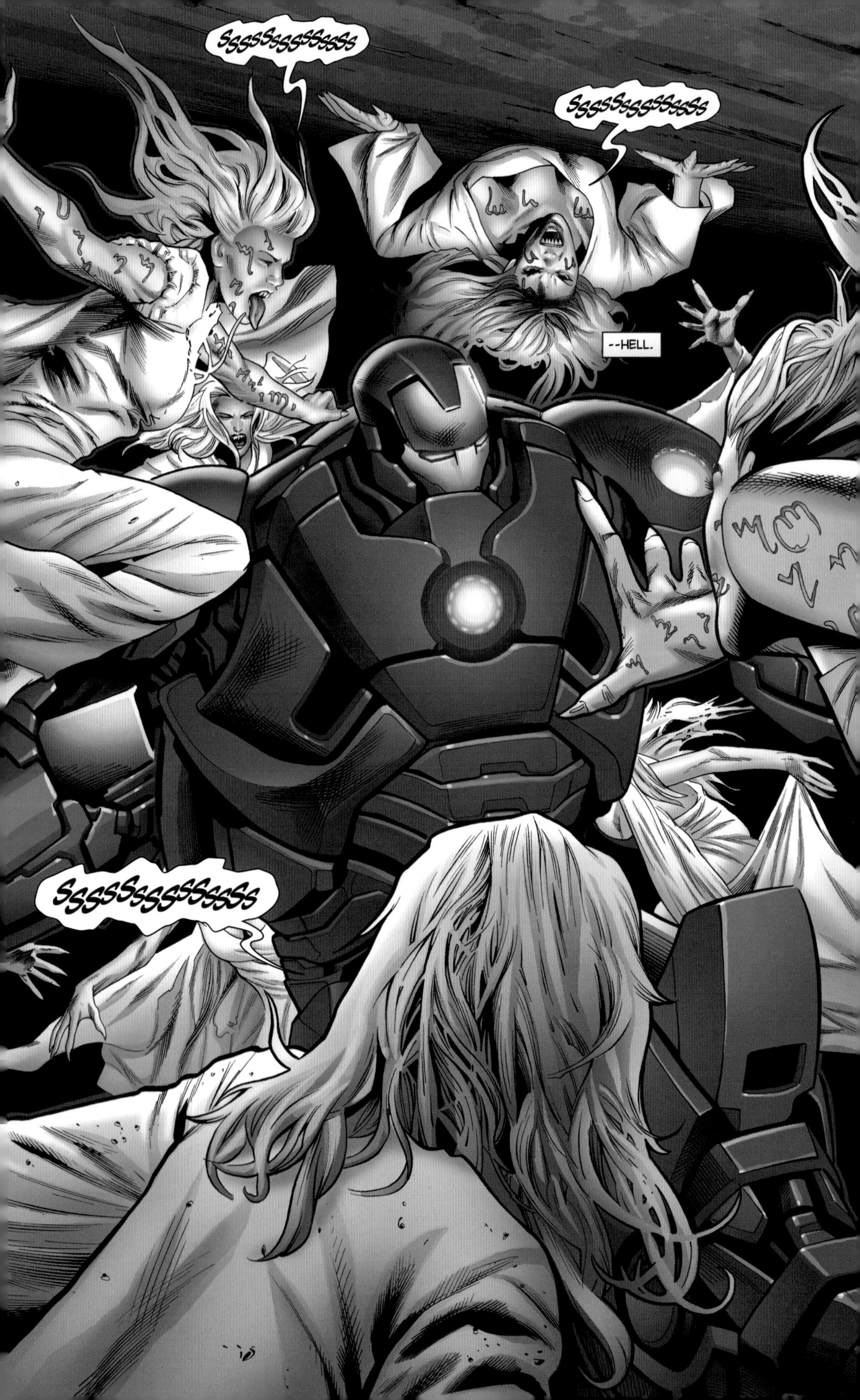
SsssSssssSSssss
SsssSssssSSssss
--HELL.
SsssSssssSSssss

HELL!

I COULD FIGHT *A* HULK IN THIS SUIT.

BUT NOT THIRTEEN.

SSSSSSSSSSSSS

NO.

GET IN HERE.

QUICKLY!

KKKRRR KK KK!

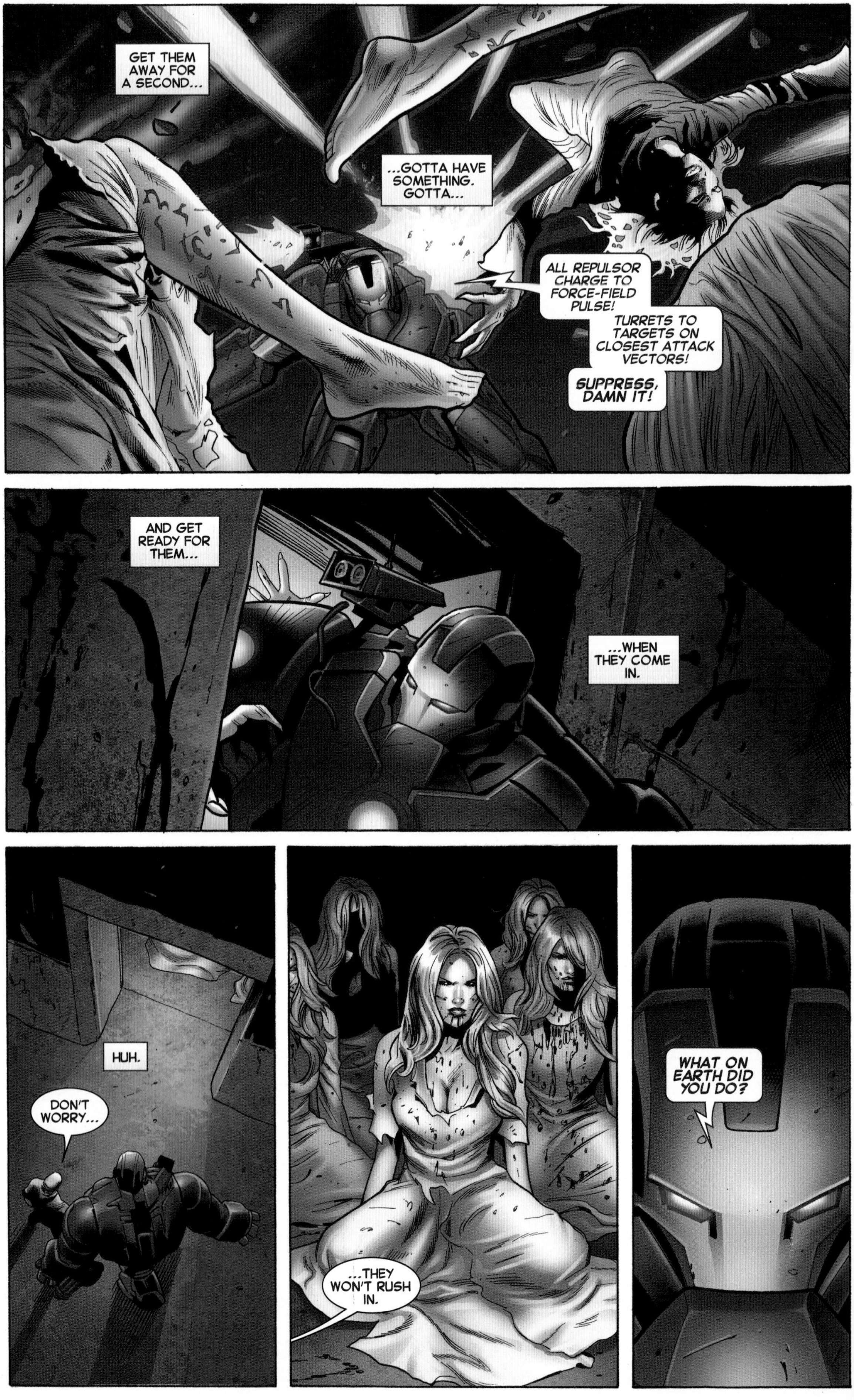
GET THEM AWAY FOR A SECOND...
...GOTTA HAVE SOMETHING. GOTTA...
ALL REPULSOR CHARGE TO FORCE-FIELD PULSE!
TURRETS TO TARGETS ON CLOSEST ATTACK VECTORS!
SUPPRESS, DAMN IT!
AND GET READY FOR THEM...
...WHEN THEY COME IN.
HUH.
DON'T WORRY...
...THEY WON'T RUSH IN.
WHAT ON EARTH DID YOU DO?

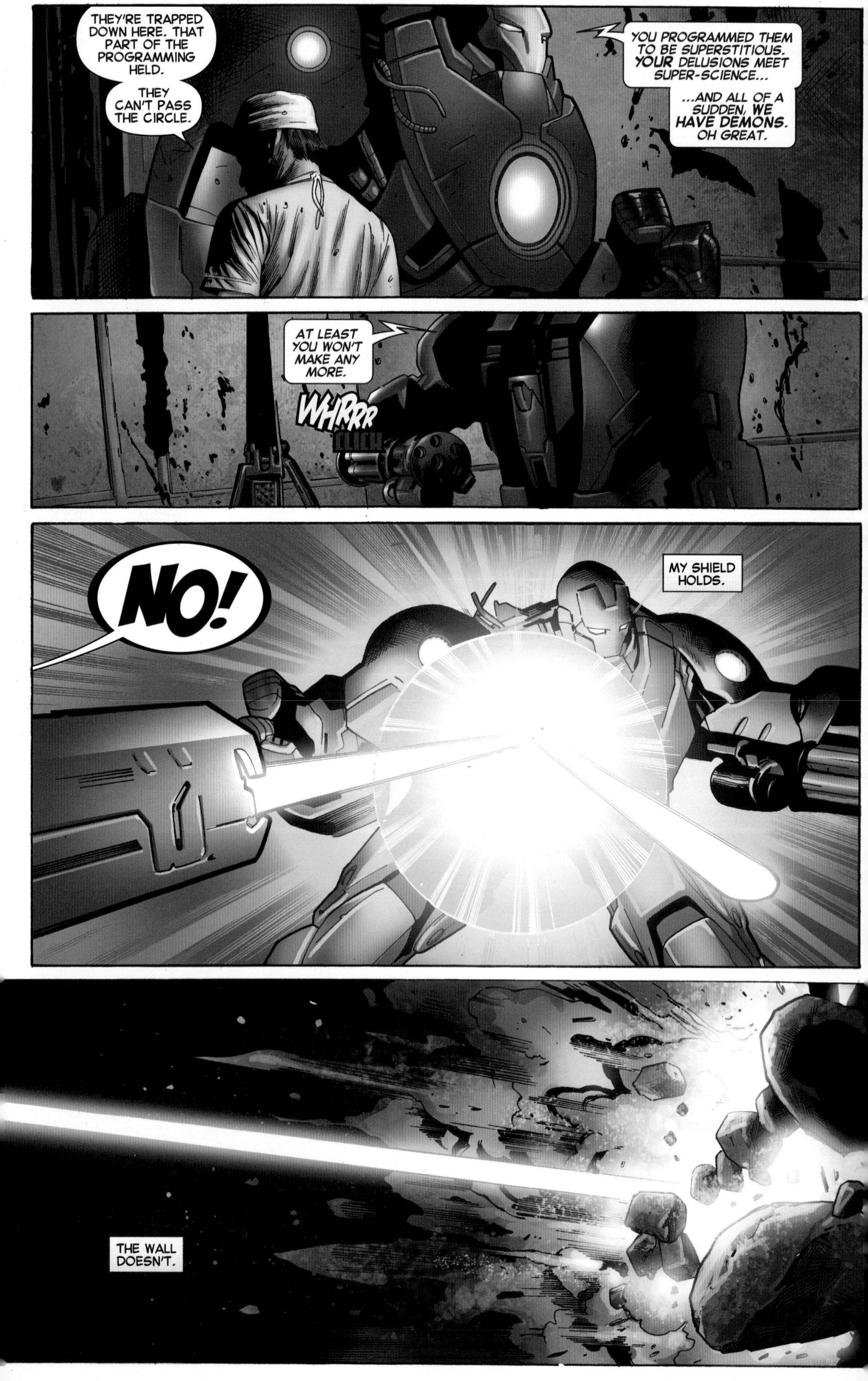
THEY'RE TRAPPED DOWN HERE. THAT PART OF THE PROGRAMMING HELD.
THEY CAN'T PASS THE CIRCLE.
YOU PROGRAMMED THEM TO BE SUPERSTITIOUS. YOUR DELUSIONS MEET SUPER-SCIENCE...
...AND ALL OF A SUDDEN, WE HAVE DEMONS. OH GREAT.
AT LEAST YOU WON'T MAKE ANY MORE.
WHRRR
CLICK
NO!
MY SHIELD HOLDS.
THE WALL DOESN'T.

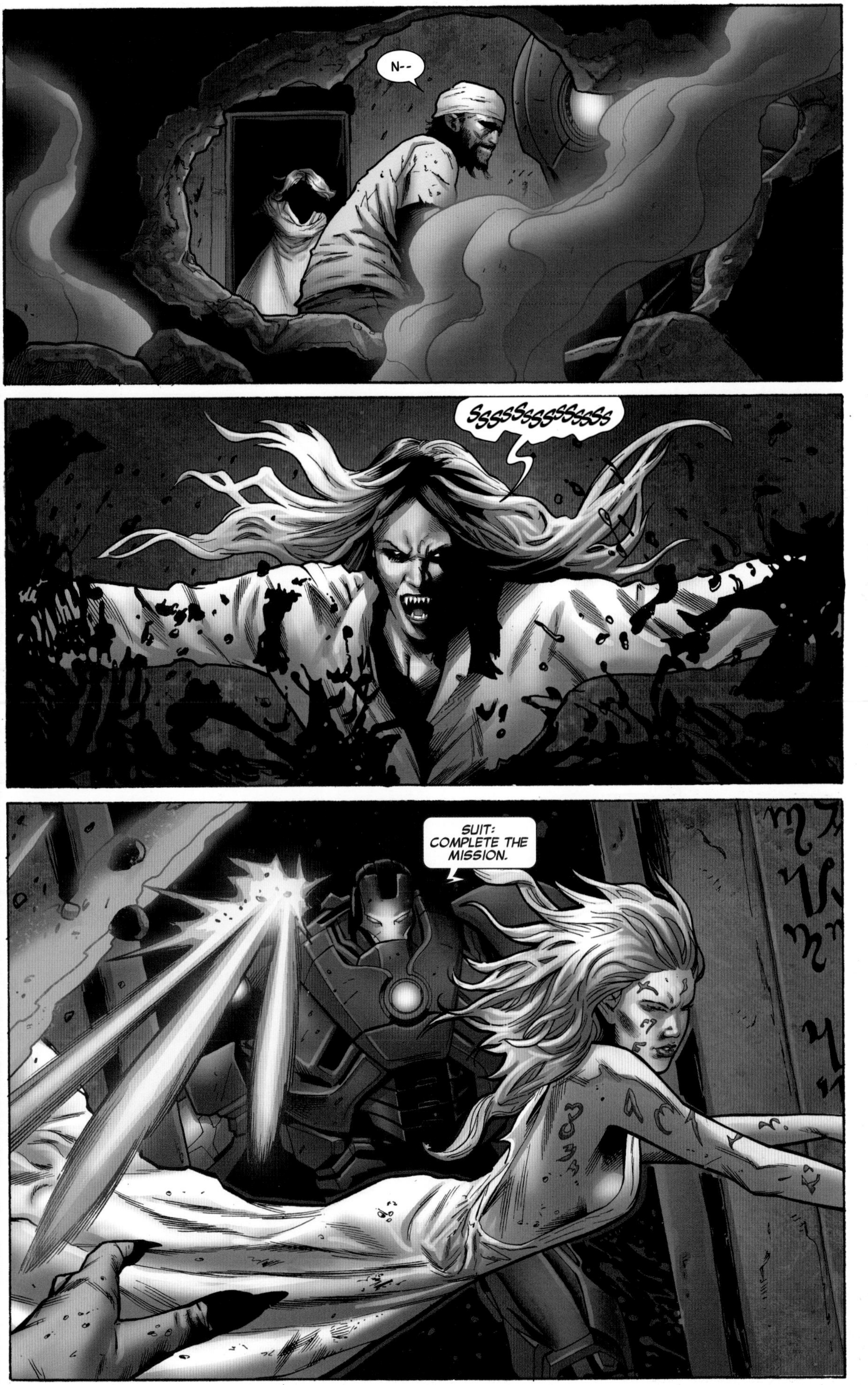
N--
SSSSSSSSSSSSSS
SUIT: COMPLETE THE MISSION.

UH-HUH.

NOW CAN I GET OUT OF HERE?

IF I BLAST A WAY STRAIGHT UP, THEY'LL FOLLOW ME INTO PARIS AND IT'S A BIBLICAL BODY COUNT.

SO I HAVE TO TRY AND FIGHT MY WAY TO ONE OF THE EXITS SEALED WITH THE WORDS.

AND THEY'LL TEAR ME APART IN THIRTY METERS TOPS.

WAIT!

SUIT: ACCESS VISUAL RECORDINGS. LOCALIZE SYMBOLS.

UH-HUH.

LASER: REPLICATE!

DO I HAVE TO?

YES, YOU DAMN WELL DO.

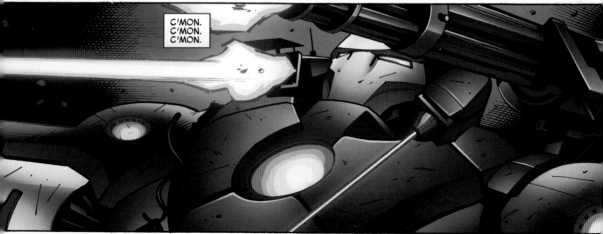

C'MON. C'MON. C'MON.

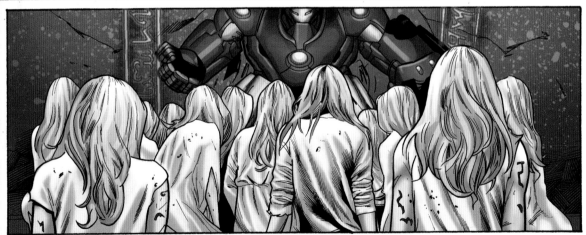

WERE THEY VOLUNTEERS? MAYBE SOME.

I'LL BET NOT ALL.

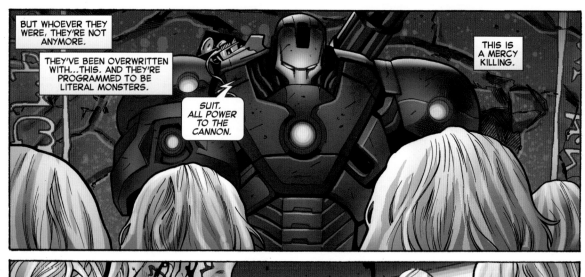

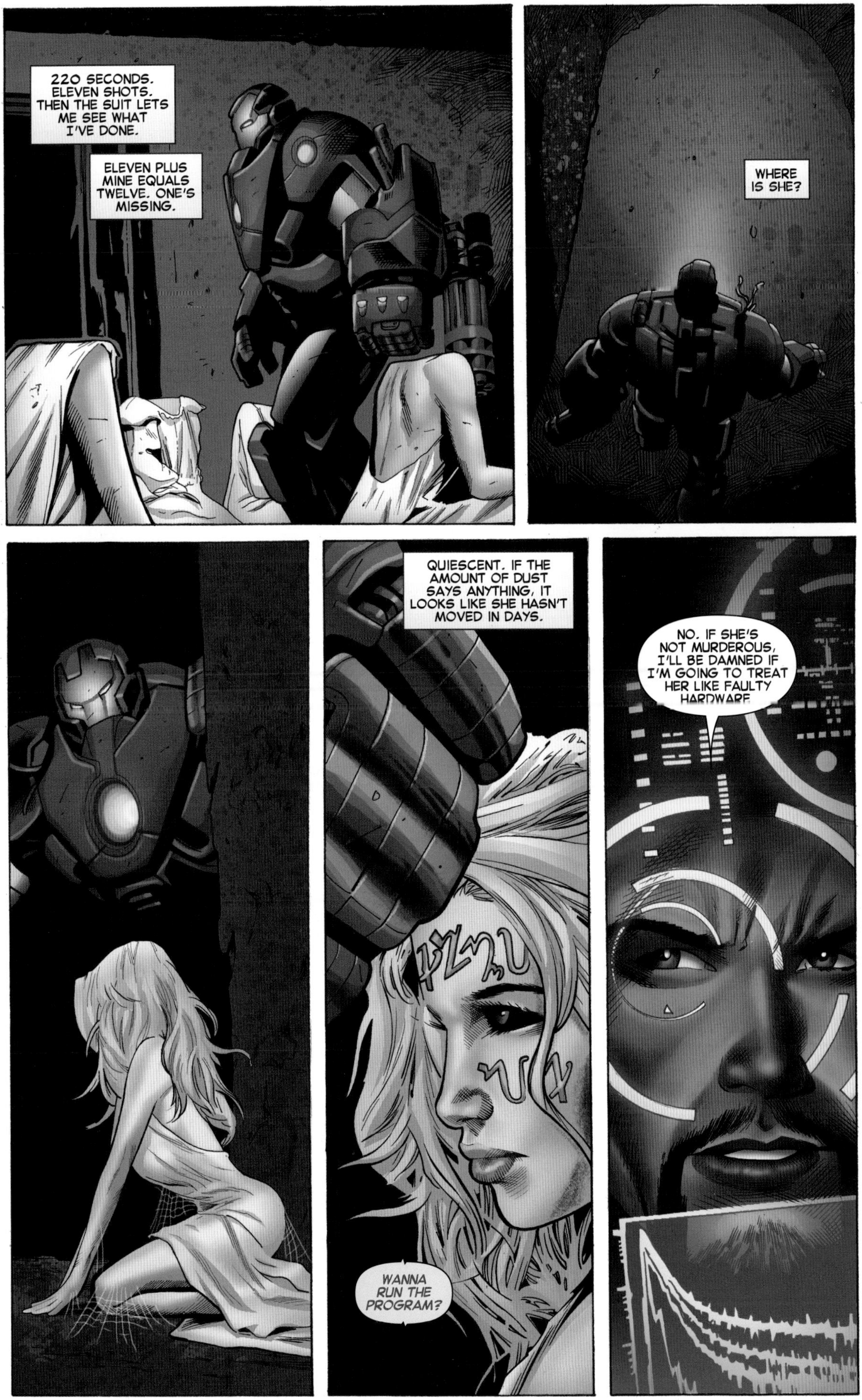
220 SECONDS. ELEVEN SHOTS. THEN THE SUIT LETS ME SEE WHAT I'VE DONE.
ELEVEN PLUS MINE EQUALS TWELVE. ONE'S MISSING.
WHERE IS SHE?
QUIESCENT. IF THE AMOUNT OF DUST SAYS ANYTHING, IT LOOKS LIKE SHE HASN'T MOVED IN DAYS.
WANNA RUN THE PROGRAM?
NO. IF SHE'S NOT MURDEROUS, I'LL BE DAMNED IF I'M GOING TO TREAT HER LIKE FAULTY HARDWARE.

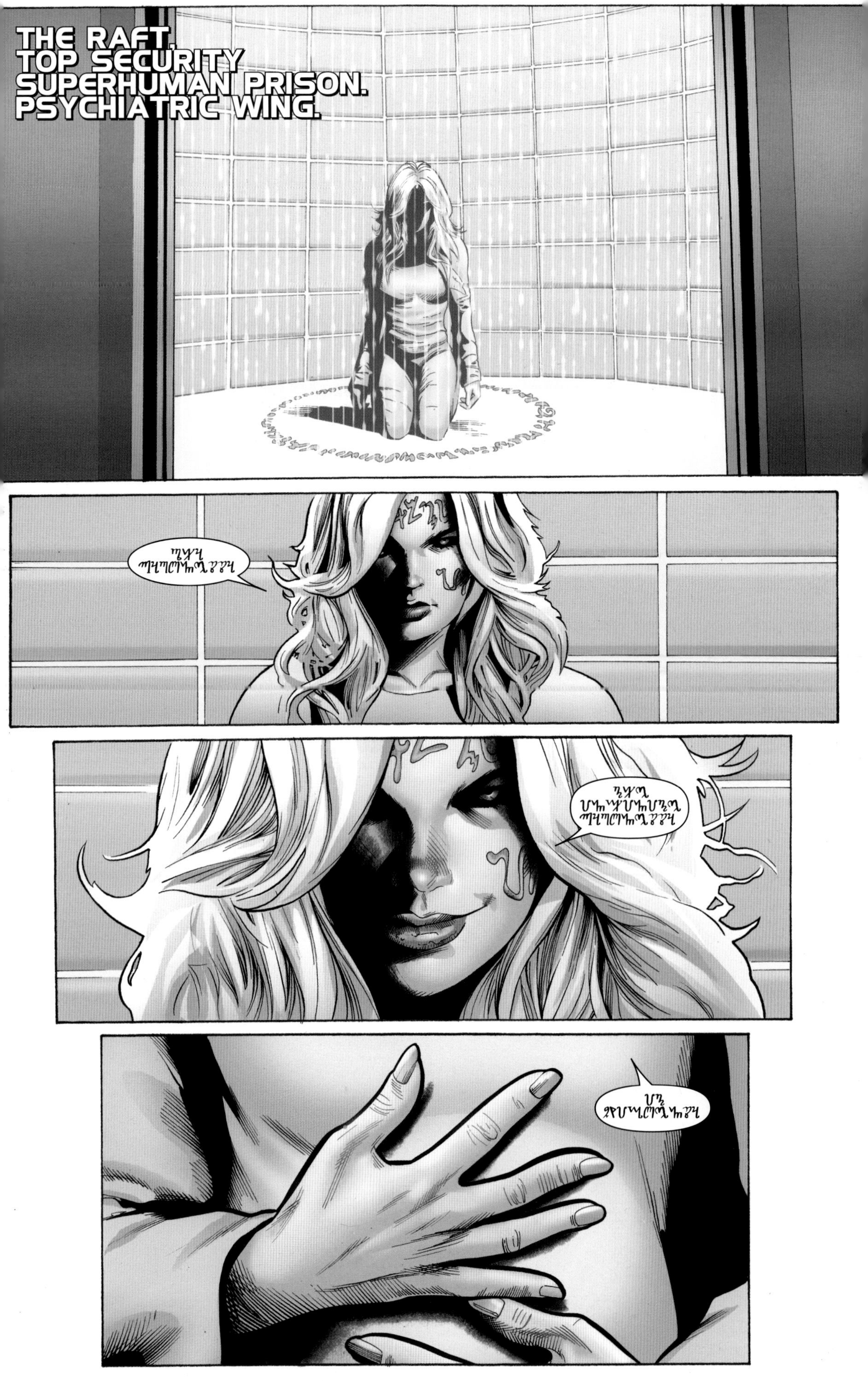
THE RAFT.
TOP SECURITY
SUPERHUMAN PRISON.
PSYCHIATRIC WING.

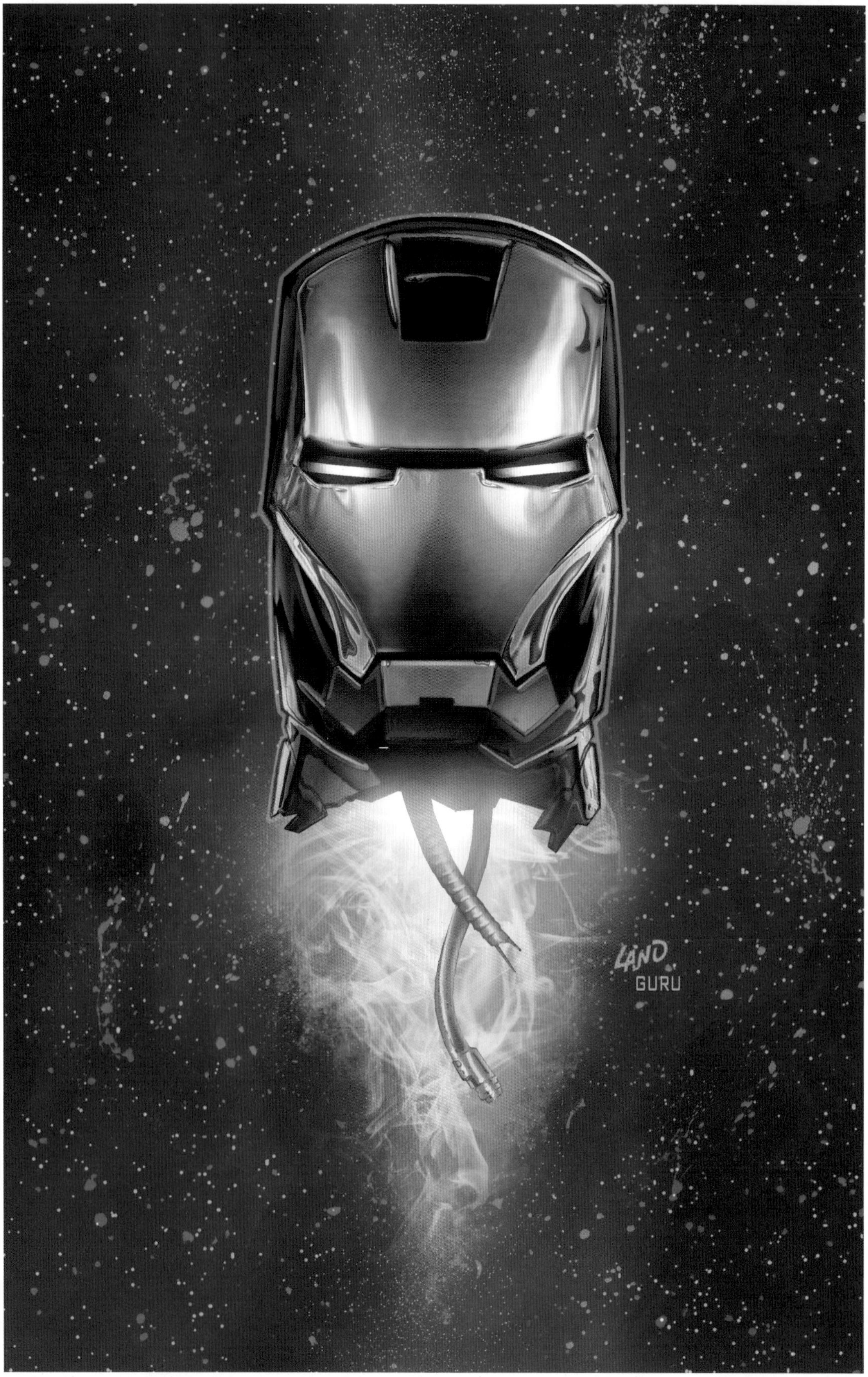
LAND
GURU

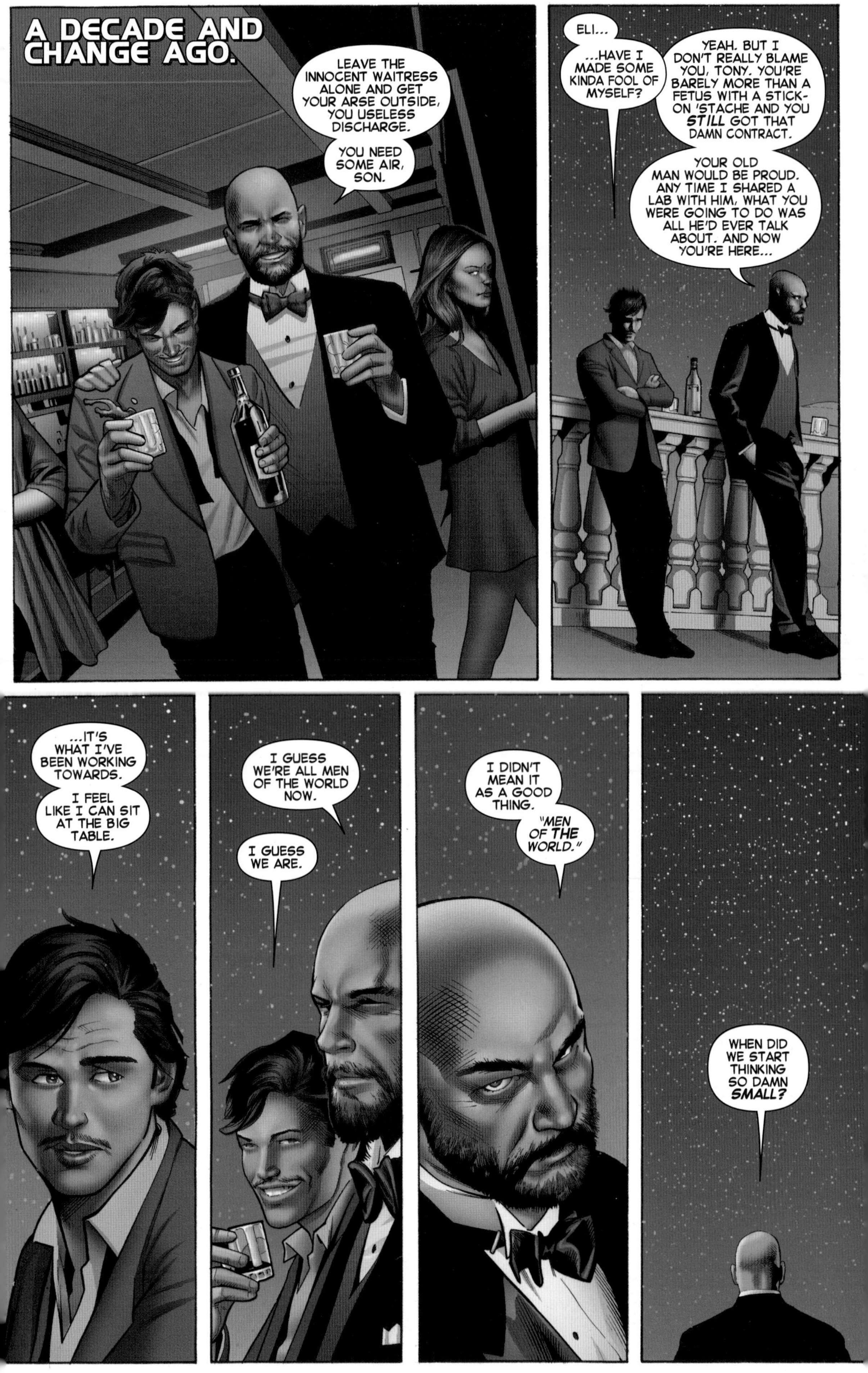

A DECADE AND CHANGE AGO.
LEAVE THE INNOCENT WAITRESS ALONE AND GET YOUR ARSE OUTSIDE, YOU USELESS DISCHARGE.
YOU NEED SOME AIR, SON.
ELI...
...HAVE I MADE SOME KINDA FOOL OF MYSELF?
YEAH. BUT I DON'T REALLY BLAME YOU, TONY. YOU'RE BARELY MORE THAN A FETUS WITH A STICK-ON 'STACHE AND YOU *STILL* GOT THAT DAMN CONTRACT.
YOUR OLD MAN WOULD BE PROUD. ANY TIME I SHARED A LAB WITH HIM, WHAT YOU WERE GOING TO DO WAS ALL HE'D EVER TALK ABOUT. AND NOW YOU'RE HERE...
...IT'S WHAT I'VE BEEN WORKING TOWARDS.
I FEEL LIKE I CAN SIT AT THE BIG TABLE.
I GUESS WE'RE ALL MEN OF THE WORLD NOW.
I GUESS WE ARE.
I DIDN'T MEAN IT AS A GOOD THING.
"MEN OF *THE* WORLD."
WHEN DID WE START THINKING SO DAMN *SMALL?*

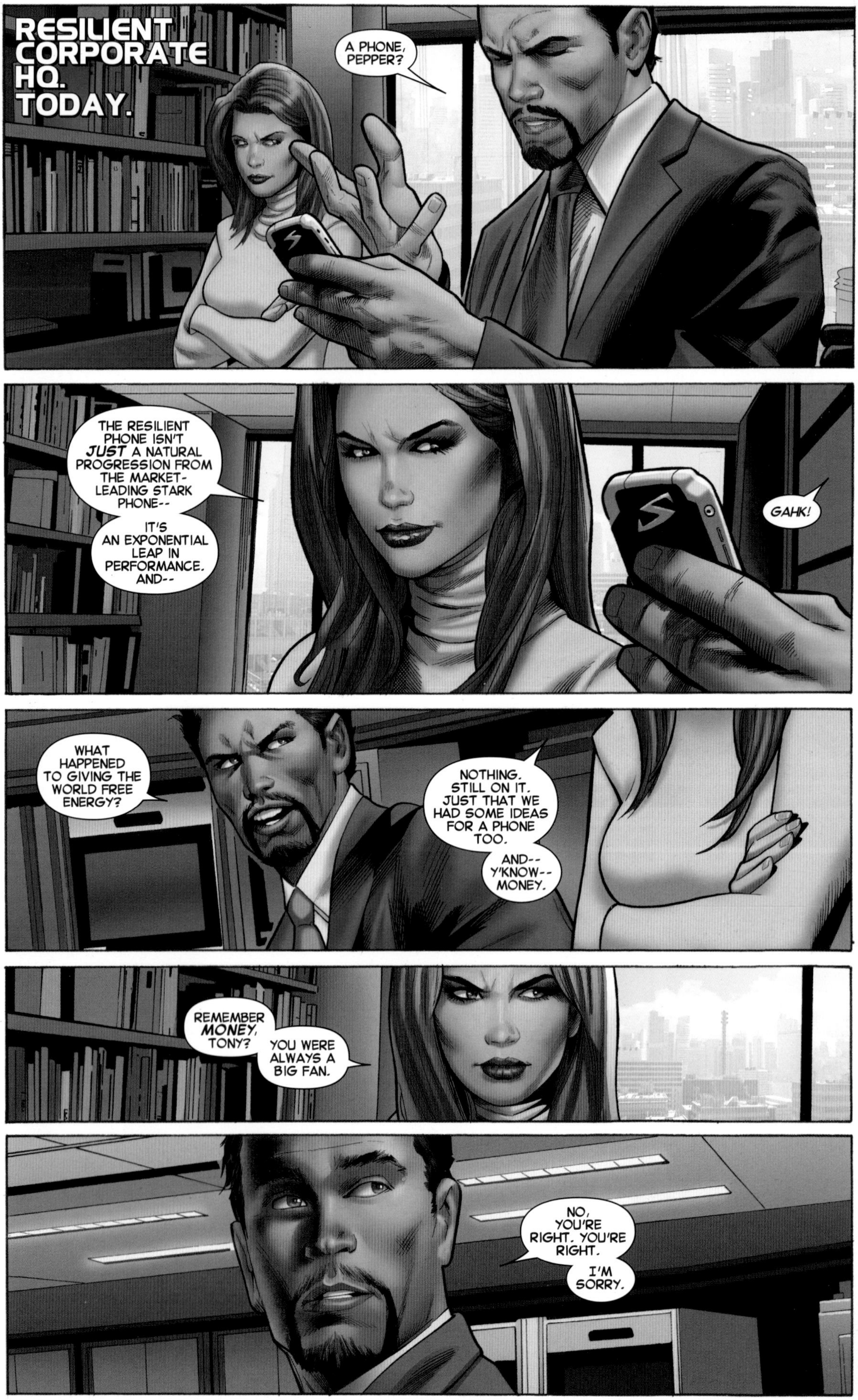
RESILIENT CORPORATE HQ. TODAY.
A PHONE, PEPPER?
THE RESILIENT PHONE ISN'T JUST A NATURAL PROGRESSION FROM THE MARKET-LEADING STARK PHONE--
IT'S AN EXPONENTIAL LEAP IN PERFORMANCE. AND--
GAHK!
WHAT HAPPENED TO GIVING THE WORLD FREE ENERGY?
NOTHING. STILL ON IT. JUST THAT WE HAD SOME IDEAS FOR A PHONE TOO.
AND--Y'KNOW--MONEY.
REMEMBER MONEY, TONY?
YOU WERE ALWAYS A BIG FAN.
NO, YOU'RE RIGHT. YOU'RE RIGHT.
I'M SORRY.

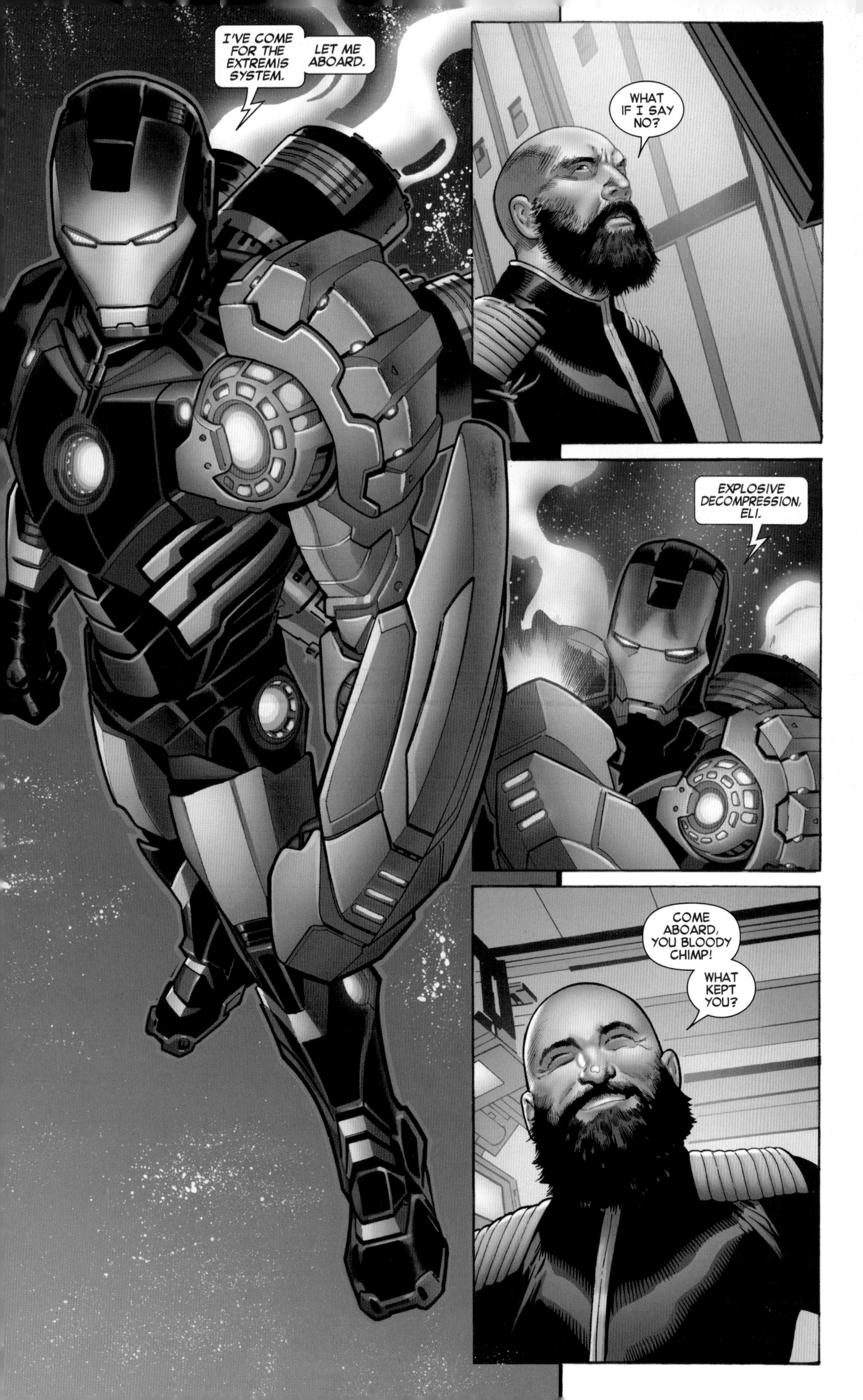
I'VE COME FOR THE EXTREMIS SYSTEM.
LET ME ABOARD.
WHAT IF I SAY NO?
EXPLOSIVE DECOMPRESSION, ELI.
COME ABOARD, YOU BLOODY CHIMP!
WHAT KEPT YOU?

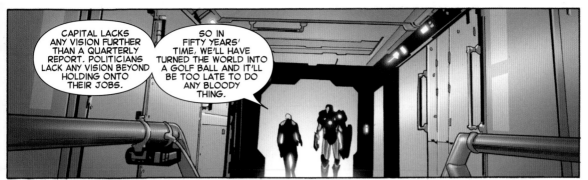

CAPITAL LACKS ANY VISION FURTHER THAN A QUARTERLY REPORT. POLITICIANS LACK ANY VISION BEYOND HOLDING ONTO THEIR JOBS.

SO IN FIFTY YEARS' TIME, WE'LL HAVE TURNED THE WORLD INTO A GOLF BALL AND IT'LL BE TOO LATE TO DO ANY BLOODY THING.

WE STOLE EVERYTHING YOU SEE AROUND HERE. EITHER THE TECH ITSELF, OR THE MONEY TO PAY FOR IT.

IF IT'S OUR ONLY OPTION, WE TAKE IT. WE HAVE TO. I'VE KNOWN THAT FOREVER.

"I STILL REMEMBER THE MOON LANDINGS. ALL GRAINY AND *STILL* BRIGHTER THAN ANYTHING I DREAMED OF.

"AND THAT WAS *IT*.

"FORGET YOU SUPER HEROES. THAT'S AS FAR AS *WE* GOT."

ALL THAT'S GOING TO CHANGE.

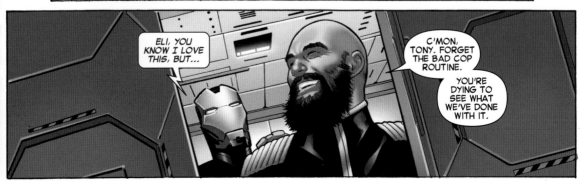

ELI, YOU KNOW I LOVE THIS, BUT...

C'MON, TONY. FORGET THE BAD COP ROUTINE.

YOU'RE DYING TO SEE WHAT WE'VE DONE WITH IT.

FORGET THE BIG THINGS LIKE RADIATION AND THE VACUUM.

WE STAY UP HERE? WE LOSE MUSCLE MASS. LOSE SKELETAL DENSITY. IN A FEW MONTHS, YOUR EYES ARE SQUISHED AND YOU'RE NOT SEEING PROPER.

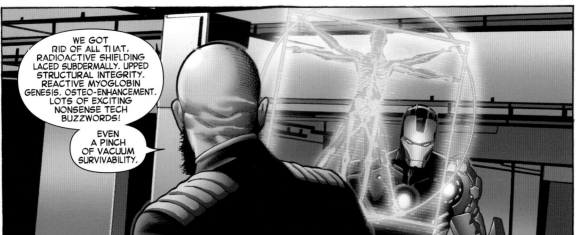

WE GOT RID OF ALL THAT. RADIOACTIVE SHIELDING LACED SUBDERMALLY. UPPED STRUCTURAL INTEGRITY. REACTIVE MYOGLOBIN GENESIS. OSTEO-ENHANCEMENT. LOTS OF EXCITING NONSENSE TECH BUZZWORDS!

EVEN A PINCH OF VACUUM SURVIVABILITY.

WE WERE MADE FOR EARTH. BUT NOW, THANKS TO EXTREMIS, WE GET TO DECIDE WHAT WE WANT TO BE.

WE GET TO BE GROWN-UPS.

YOU'RE ALL UPGRADED NOW, SO...WHY DO YOU NEED THE KIT?

THE STANDARD DOSE IS HANDY, BUT IT'S MAINLY A BASAL STATE WE CAN TWIST WITH THE OTHER EXTREMIS MODS WE'RE WORKING ON.

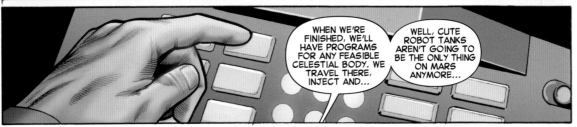

WHEN WE'RE FINISHED, WE'LL HAVE PROGRAMS FOR ANY FEASIBLE CELESTIAL BODY. WE TRAVEL THERE, INJECT AND...

WELL, CUTE ROBOT TANKS AREN'T GOING TO BE THE ONLY THING ON MARS ANYMORE...

AND I LET THEM MAKE THEIR PLAY, AS THEM GOING FOR THEIR GUNS MAKES ME THE GOOD GUY.

YOU GET TO KEEP WHAT'S INSIDE YOU. YOU AND YOURS CAN NOW STAY IN SPACE *PERMANENTLY.*

YOU CAN DO INCREDIBLE THINGS WITH THAT.

AND REALLY? YOU DIDN'T WANT IT LIKE THIS. THIS IS TOO EASY, ELI.

WE HAVE TO CLIMB THIS MOUNTAIN BY OURSELVES.

WE DON'T DO IT BECAUSE IT'S EASY.

WE DO IT BECAUSE IT'S HARD.

I'M RIGHT. I KNOW I AM.

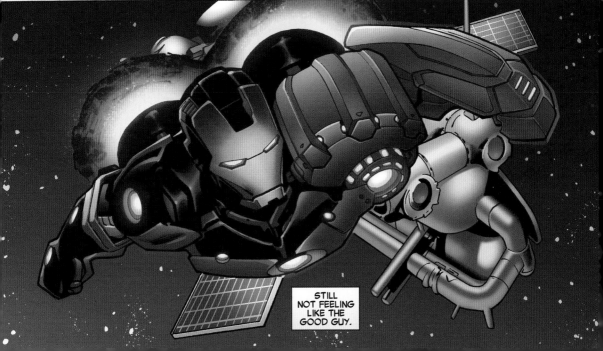

STILL NOT FEELING LIKE THE GOOD GUY.

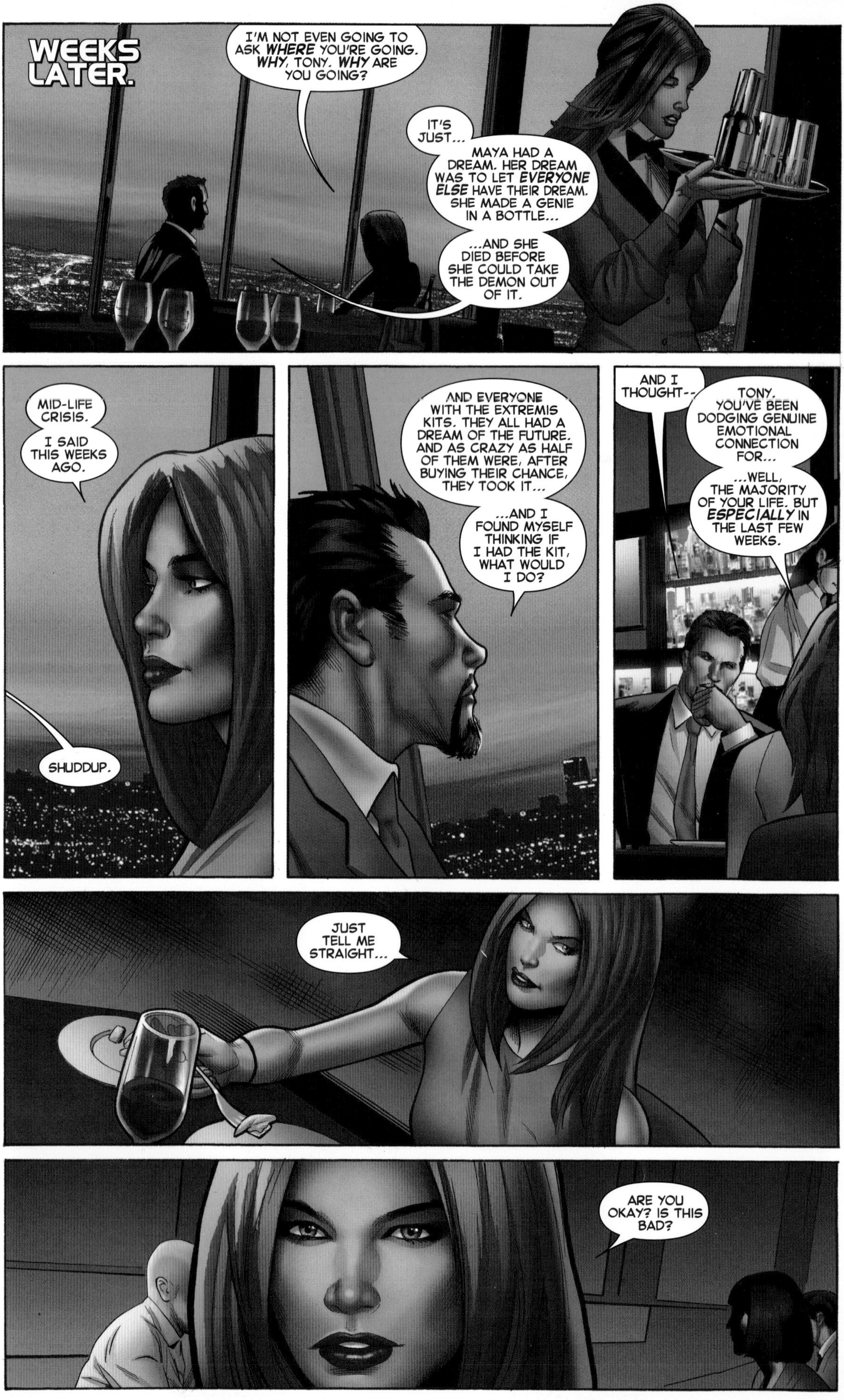
WEEKS LATER.
I'M NOT EVEN GOING TO ASK WHERE YOU'RE GOING. WHY, TONY. WHY ARE YOU GOING?
IT'S JUST...
MAYA HAD A DREAM. HER DREAM WAS TO LET EVERYONE ELSE HAVE THEIR DREAM. SHE MADE A GENIE IN A BOTTLE...
...AND SHE DIED BEFORE SHE COULD TAKE THE DEMON OUT OF IT.
MID-LIFE CRISIS.
I SAID THIS WEEKS AGO.
SHUDDUP.
AND EVERYONE WITH THE EXTREMIS KITS. THEY ALL HAD A DREAM OF THE FUTURE. AND AS CRAZY AS HALF OF THEM WERE, AFTER BUYING THEIR CHANCE, THEY TOOK IT...
...AND I FOUND MYSELF THINKING IF I HAD THE KIT, WHAT WOULD I DO?
AND I THOUGHT--
TONY. YOU'VE BEEN DODGING GENUINE EMOTIONAL CONNECTION FOR...
...WELL, THE MAJORITY OF YOUR LIFE. BUT ESPECIALLY IN THE LAST FEW WEEKS.
JUST TELL ME STRAIGHT...
ARE YOU OKAY? IS THIS BAD?

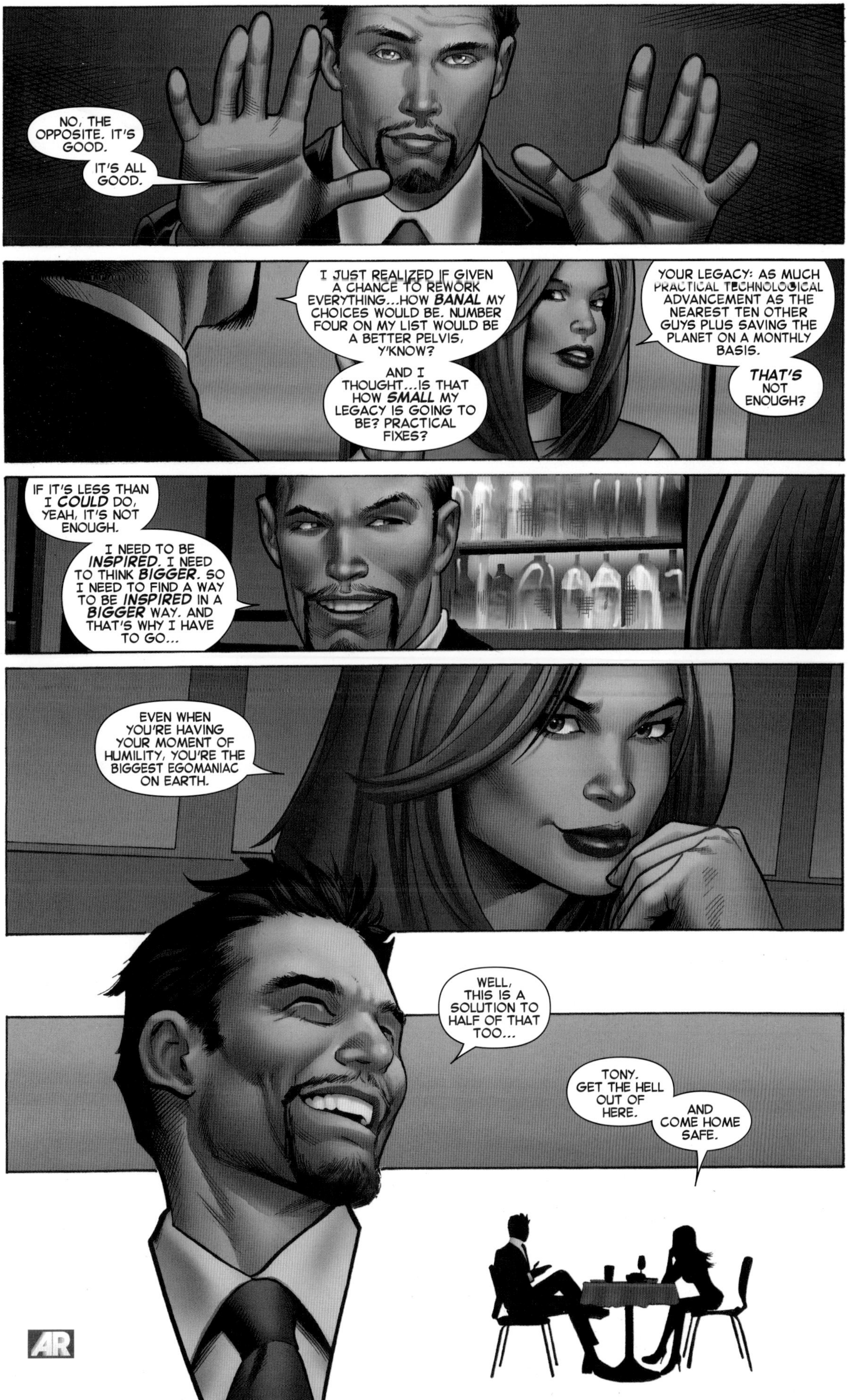
NO, THE OPPOSITE. IT'S GOOD.
IT'S ALL GOOD.
I JUST REALIZED IF GIVEN A CHANCE TO REWORK EVERYTHING...HOW BANAL MY CHOICES WOULD BE. NUMBER FOUR ON MY LIST WOULD BE A BETTER PELVIS, Y'KNOW?
AND I THOUGHT...IS THAT HOW SMALL MY LEGACY IS GOING TO BE? PRACTICAL FIXES?
YOUR LEGACY: AS MUCH PRACTICAL TECHNOLOGICAL ADVANCEMENT AS THE NEAREST TEN OTHER GUYS PLUS SAVING THE PLANET ON A MONTHLY BASIS.
THAT'S NOT ENOUGH?
IF IT'S LESS THAN I COULD DO, YEAH, IT'S NOT ENOUGH.
I NEED TO BE INSPIRED. I NEED TO THINK BIGGER. SO I NEED TO FIND A WAY TO BE INSPIRED IN A BIGGER WAY. AND THAT'S WHY I HAVE TO GO...
EVEN WHEN YOU'RE HAVING YOUR MOMENT OF HUMILITY, YOU'RE THE BIGGEST EGOMANIAC ON EARTH.
WELL, THIS IS A SOLUTION TO HALF OF THAT TOO...
TONY. GET THE HELL OUT OF HERE.
AND COME HOME SAFE.

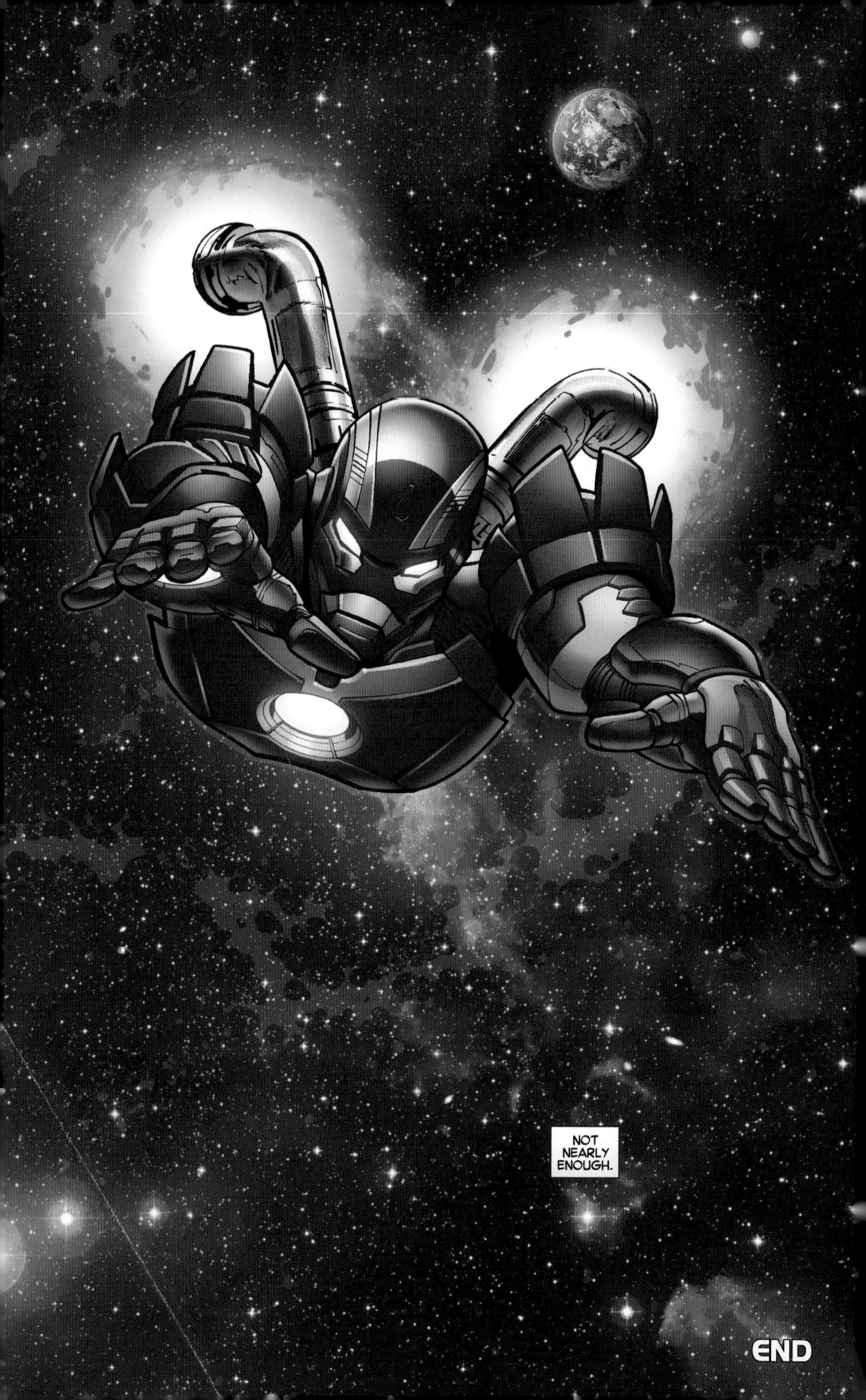
NOT NEARLY ENOUGH.
END

IRON MAN™

Variant Cover Gallery

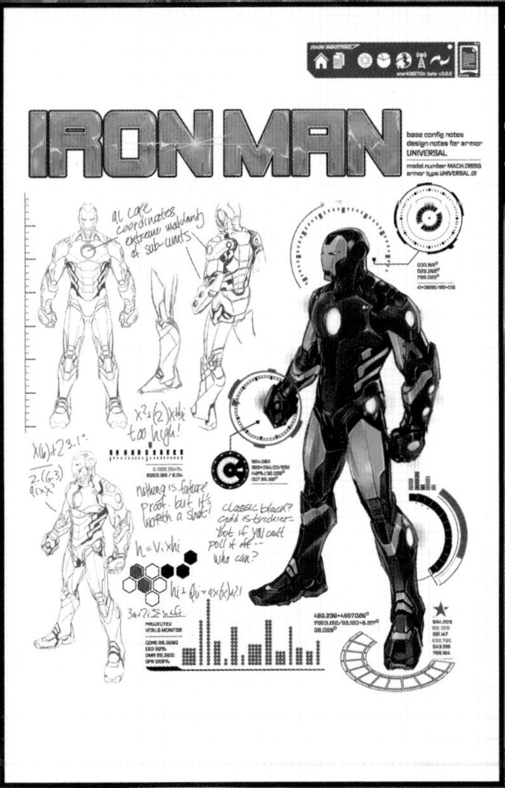

IRON MAN
base config notes
design notes for armor
UNIVERSAL

Iron Man #1
By Carlo Pagulayan

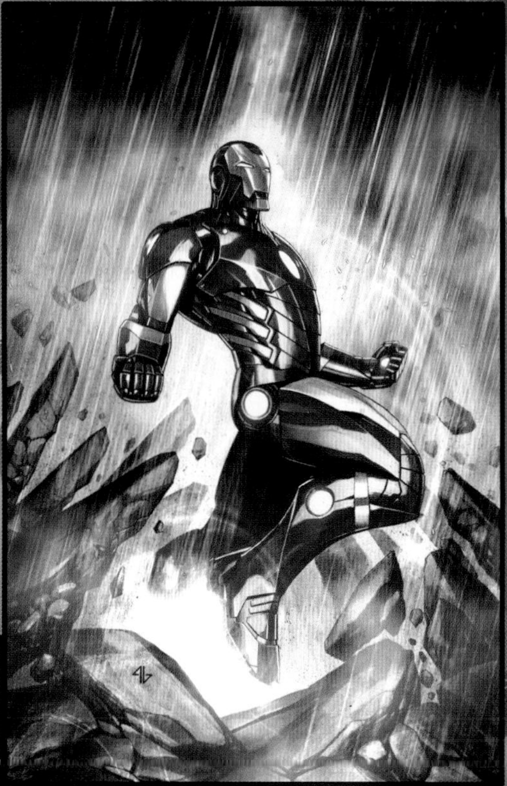

Iron Man #1
By Adi Granov

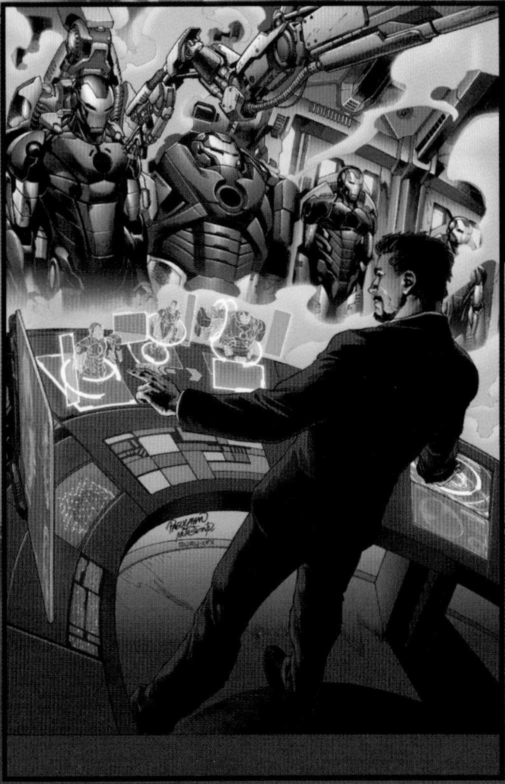

Iron Man #1 (Hastings Variant)
By Greg Land

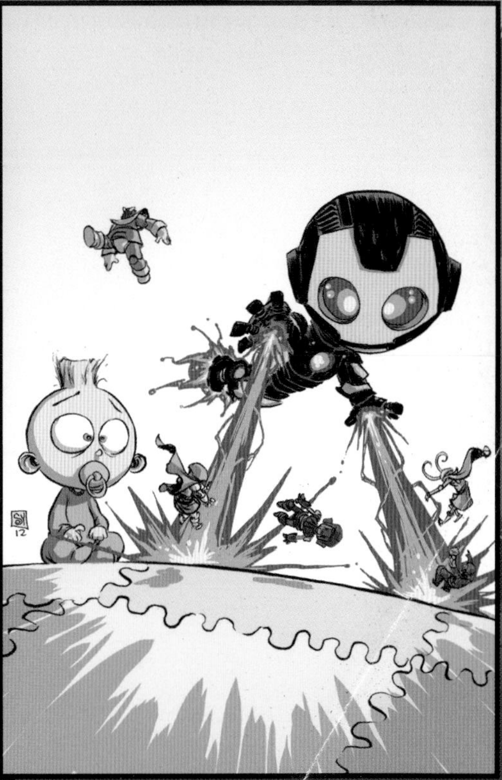

Iron Man #1
By Skott Young

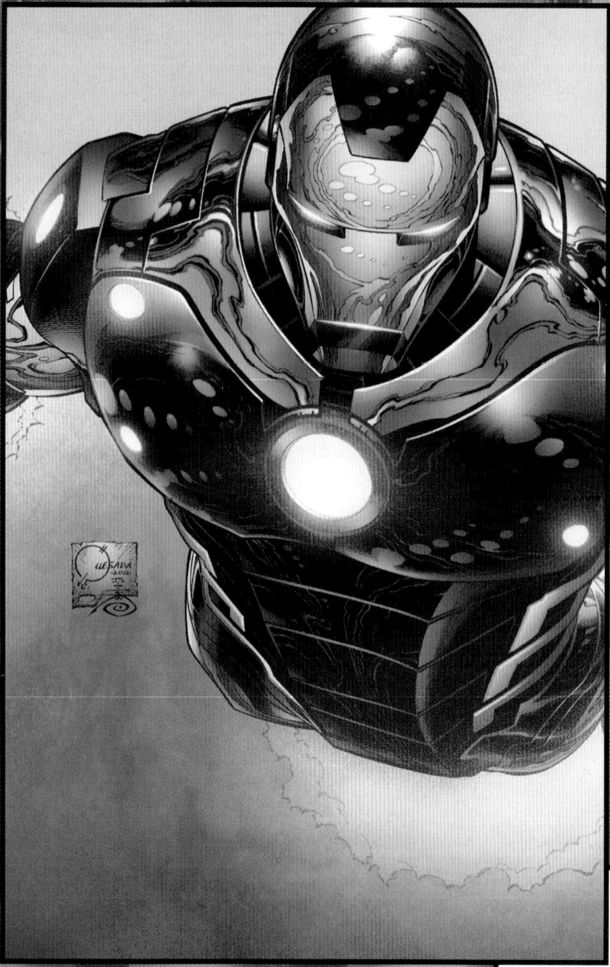

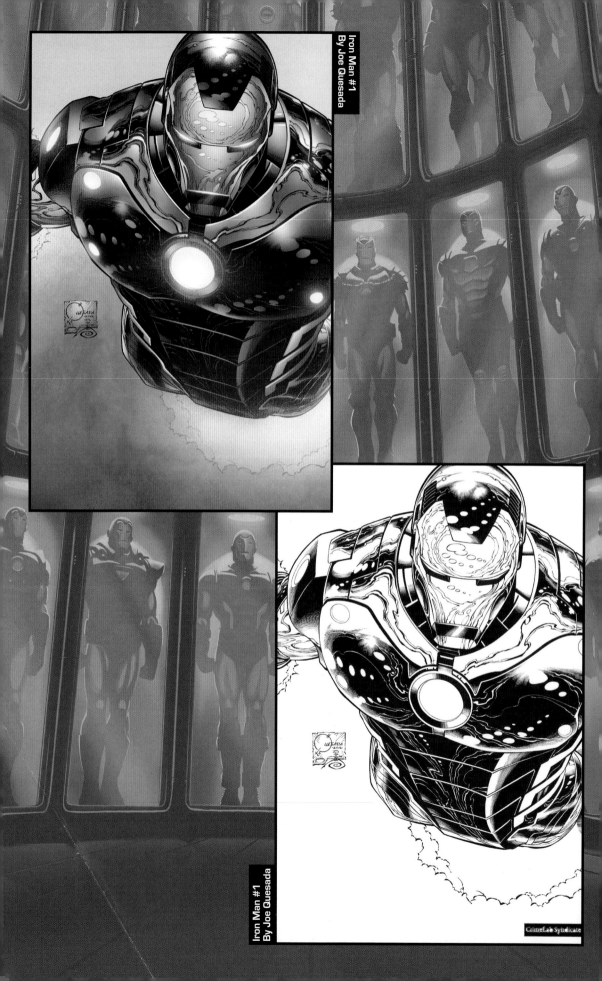

Iron Man #1
By Joe Quesada

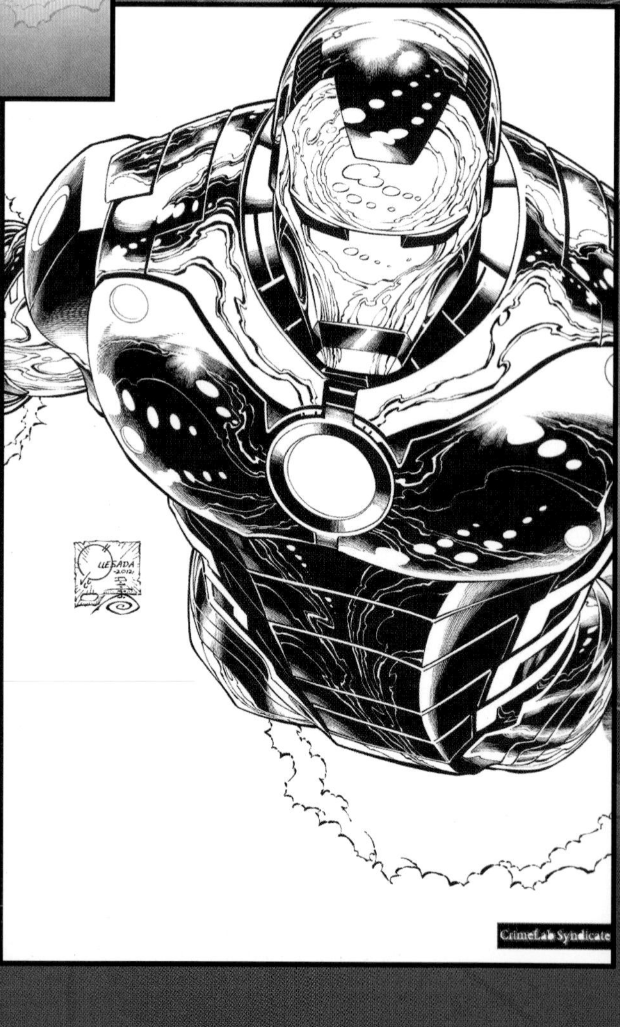

Iron Man #1
By Joe Quesada

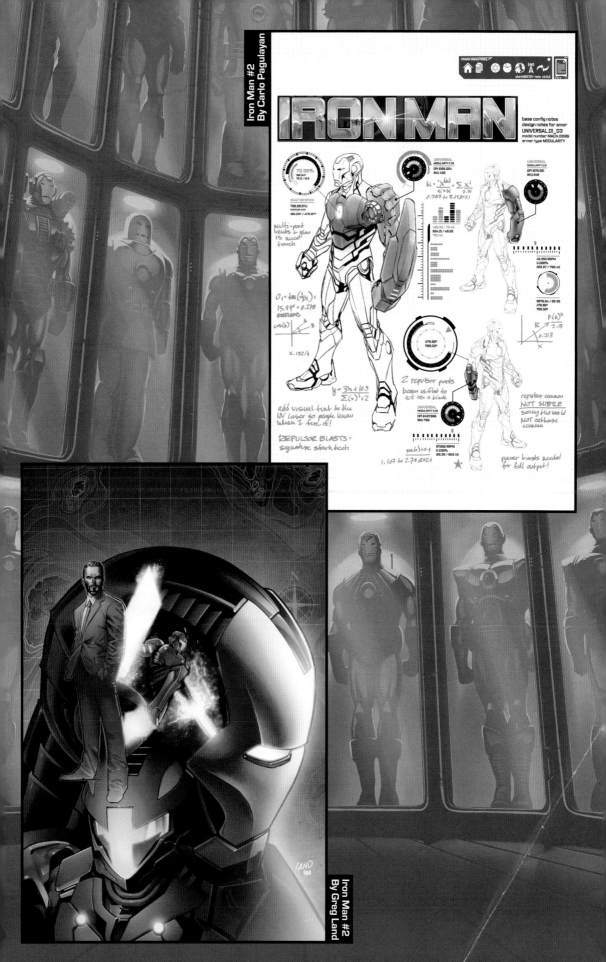

Iron Man #2
By Carlo Pagulayan

Iron Man #2
By Greg Land

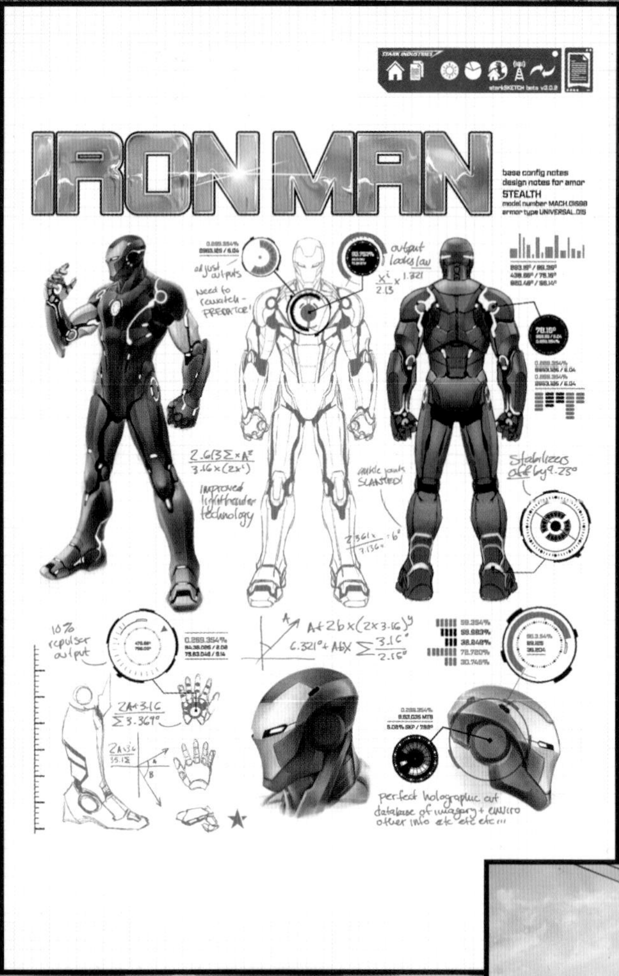
IRON MAN
base config notes
design notes for amor
STEALTH
output looks low
adjust outputs
need to rewatch - PREDATOR!
improved lightbender technology
ankle joints SLANTED!
Stabilizers off by 9.23°
10% repulsor output

Iron Man #3
By Carlo Pagulayan

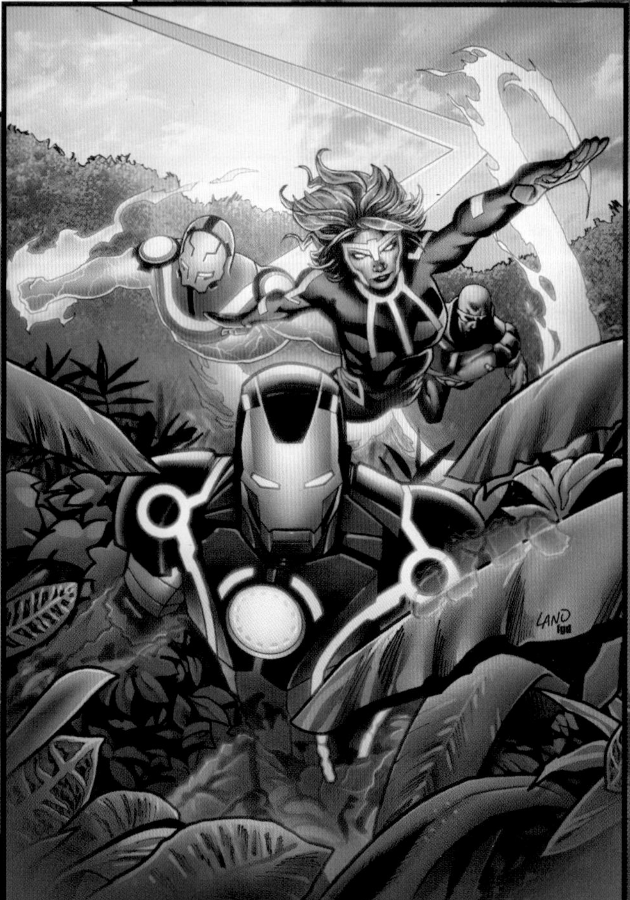
LAND

Iron Man #3
By Greg Land

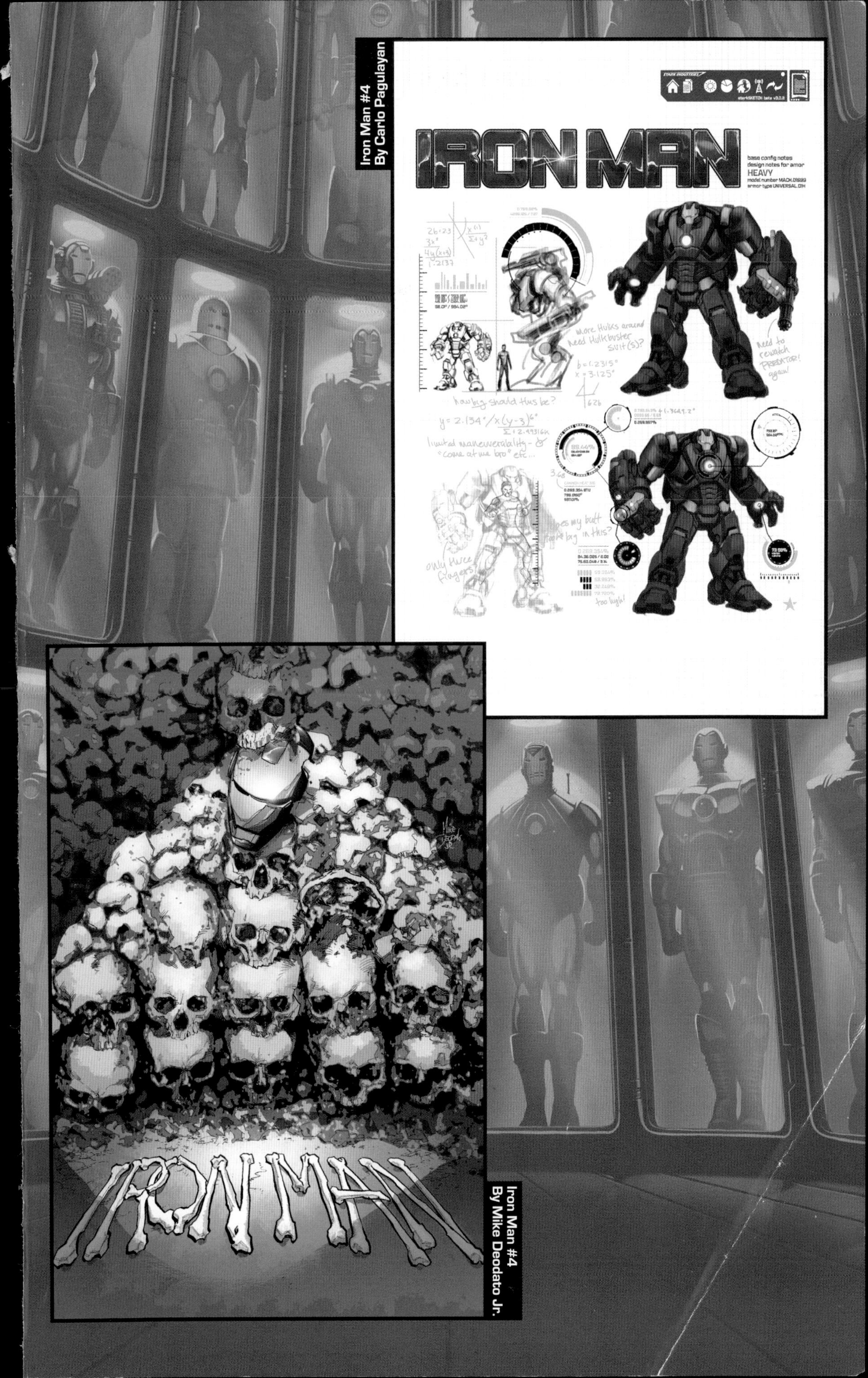

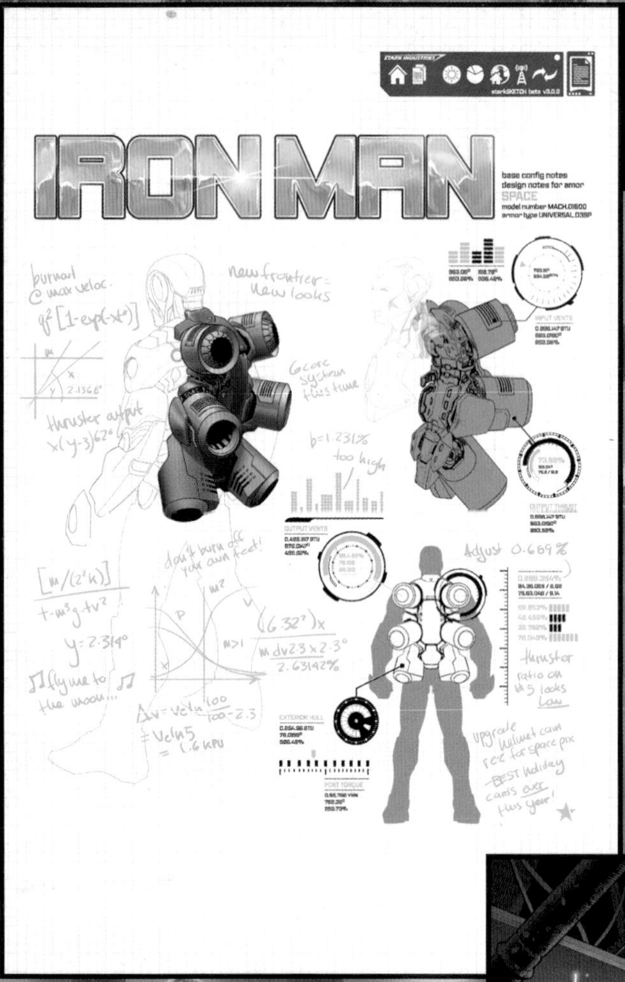
IRON MAN
base config notes
design notes for amor
SPACE
model number MACH.01600
armor type UNIVERSAL.038P
burnout @ max veloc.
new frontier = new looks
thruster output
don't burn off your own feet!
Adjust 0.669 %
fly me to the moon...
thruster ratio on M5 looks Low
BEST holiday cards ever this year!

Iron Man #5
By Carlo Pagulayan

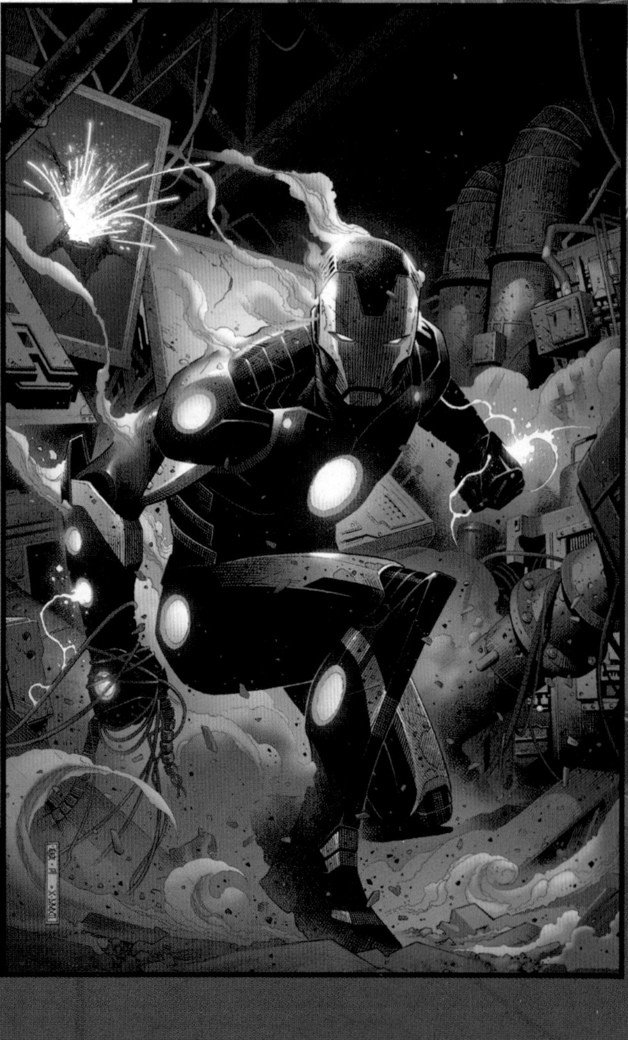

Iron Man #5
By Jim Cheung

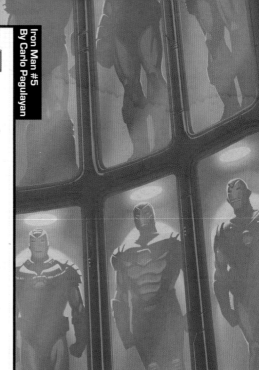

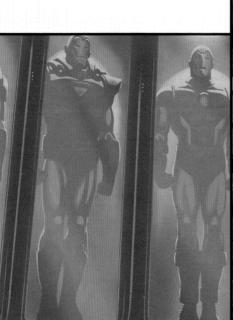